Parents' Guide

Table of Contents

Introduction

The Greatest Gift 2
Your Child and the Standards 3
Assessing Students
Occurs in a Variety of Ways. 4
Guiding Your Child to
Better Grades 5

K Kindergarten

Language Arts. 8
Math 10
Science 12
Geography. 14
History. 16

1 First Grade

Language Arts. 20
Math 22
Science 24
Geography. 26
History. 28

2 Second Grade

Language Arts. 32
Math 34
Science 36
Geography. 38
History. 40

3 Third Grade

Language Arts. 44
Math 46
Science 48
Geography. 50
History. 52

4 Fourth Grade

Language Arts. 56
Math 58
Science 61
Geography. 64
History. 66

5 Fifth Grade

Language Arts. 70
Math 72
Science 74
Geography. 77
History. 79

6 Sixth Grade

Language Arts. 84
Math 86
Science 89
Geography. 91
History. 94

© Summit Learning - *A Steck-Vaughn Company*
Reproduction prohibited

Introduction

The Greatest Gift

"The greatest gift we can give our children is a good education."

These are words all parents should take to heart. With a good education, our children can become vital, productive members of the community.

But what is a good education? What are the criteria? Of course, there are differences of opinion regarding just what a good education is. In the United States, a well-rounded approach to learning is used.

To this end, educational standards have been developed. These standards are statements of what students should know and be able to do in each subject area. Standards are high and consistent expectations for all students.

This Parents' Guide to Standards lists subject areas for each grade level, with standards appropriate for that grade level. Under each standard you will find statements of what students should know or be able to do at that grade level.

Who Determined These Standards?

Over the last few decades, most states have developed academic standards for their students. This book does not present the standards from any particular state. Instead, the standards in this book are meant to be general guidelines or what is typically expected of a student in a certain grade level. Parents should use these standards as a measuring stick to gauge their children's academic progress.

Most local school districts have also set up educational standards and assessment schedules. Parents should check with their local district for specific standards and assessments used in their children's school.

How Do I Know How Well My Child Is Progressing?

Students' academic progress is monitored in several ways. Teachers use classroom activities and assessments that help to show if students are meeting or exceeding established standards. The results are used to make decisions about students' instructional needs.

Most school districts also administer district, state, and national tests to students in various grade levels. Many state tests include reading and mathematics "level tests" and a writing assessment. These tests reflect established standards and are currently being used at most grade levels.

Reports summarizing students' test results are usually sent home to parents at the end of the grading period or school year.

Again, parents should check with their local district to see what sort of assessment tests are used in their children's school.

What If My Child Doesn't Meet the Standards?

Current assessments are based on expected levels of student performance. These assessments indicate how well your child is performing on each of the standards. If your child is not performing at an expected level, the school will share that information with you and work with you to address any performance concerns to improve student learning.

Options for such students may include tutoring, extra help during extended learning times (outside the school day or year), practice work to complete at home, parent help, remedial instruction, peer tutoring, mentoring, computer-assisted education, informal or formal assessment of individual needs, and/or summer school.

INTRODUCTION

Your Child and the Standards

What Is the Relationship of Performance on Standards and a Graduation Diploma?

Most states have set performance levels for certain core standards, such as reading and writing, oral communication, mathematics, and science in order for students to receive a graduation diploma. Check with your local high school to see what kind of assessment students must pass to graduate.

How Do These Standards Apply to a Child with Special Needs?

Some students are identified as having special education needs. For these special education students, the standards may be modified, accommodations may be made, or the standards might be waived, depending on the needs of the student. Special education students are expected to meet the standards written for them in their own special program.

The needs of students whose performance exceeds standards are also addressed through various program options available in local districts or schools.

Will Standards Improve Education?

To achieve a good education, all students should learn and perform at high levels. To keep our students competitive and to get the most from our investment in education, most states have adopted rigorous expectations for what students should know and be able to do. By providing students, parents, and teachers with clear and consistent expectations across all of our schools, we increase the likelihood that students will perform at even higher levels than they have in the past.

With the adoption of standards, the focus of education becomes not just what teachers teach but also what students learn. As teachers focus their classroom efforts on students meeting and exceeding standards, schools can support student learning by helping teachers:

- apply effective instructional practices,
- use assessments more extensively to monitor student progress and to direct instruction,
- design and implement interventions for students needing more help to achieve standards or who are ready to work at more advanced levels,
- and use technology to help students achieve standards.

Schools can also focus on helping students see that what they learn in school is important to their daily lives and career goals.

How Can I Obtain More Information about Standards?

Contact your child's classroom teacher to learn more about classroom standards and your student's progress and ways in which you can provide supporting activities for your child.

Introduction

Assessing Students Occurs in a Variety of Ways

Classroom Assessments

Because teachers can use a variety of tests (multiple choice, open-ended, essay, performance tasks, observation checklists, demonstrations) and assess frequently, classroom assessments provide the most in-depth information about how well your child is meeting or exceeding standards. Classroom assessment is the most diagnostic in nature. It is also the best measure of a student's academic growth. For these reasons, the most important kind of assessment is that done in the classroom.

Student progress at the classroom level is reported through report cards and parent conferences.

District and State Assessments

Most states and local school districts also use some sort of assessments to judge student progress. These assessments vary, so contact your local school to see what sort of state and district assessments are required of students.

Norm-Referenced Tests

Norm-Referenced Tests are national tests that are written for use in any state or district. For this reason, they are not necessarily aligned with specific state or district standards.

Norm-Referenced Tests include:
- ❏ Iowa Test of Basic Skills (ITBS)
- ❏ California Achievement Test
- ❏ Metropolitan Achievement Test
- ❏ Preliminary Scholastic Achievement Test (PSAT)
- ❏ Scholastic Achievement Test (SAT)
- ❏ American College Test (ACT)

These national tests are "normed" using a national sample of students. They focus on skills and knowledge generally taught in a grade level across the country. Typically, such tests are multiple choice, and they measure skills or knowledge in general subject areas.

Results from these tests indicate how your child's scores compare with those of students across the nation.

Guiding Your Child to Better Grades

What Can Parents Do to Help Students Meet Standards?

Teachers work hard to educate our children. But parents must play an active role in their children's education, too. There are many things that you as parents can do to help your children gain a good education.

- ❏ Provide a quiet place for your child to study or do homework. Make sure your child has all the supplies necessary to complete the work.
- ❏ Set a time for your child to study or do homework. This will help your child to manage time better.
- ❏ Go over homework directions together. Make sure your child understands what he or she is supposed to do.
- ❏ Give help when needed, but remember that homework is your child's responsibility.
- ❏ Check the homework when it is done. Go over any parts your child may have had trouble completing.
- ❏ Help your child study for tests by asking sample questions or going over the material to be covered in the test.
- ❏ Review your child's schoolwork, and note improvements as well as problems.

A Final Note

Remember that standards are useless unless there is a desire to achieve them. Promote learning in your children. Help them to become better acquainted with the world around them. Encourage them to do their best in all their endeavors, both in school and outside it. Talk to your children about their lessons. Ask questions. You might even learn something new!

KINDERGARTEN

Language Arts
Math
Science
Geography
History

PARENTS' GUIDE TO STANDARDS

 KINDERGARTEN

 **LANGUAGE ARTS**

Standard 1 – Reading

Students read and understand a variety of materials.

- ❏ Connect the written word with personal experience.

- ❏ Explore language as a variety of materials are read: rhymes and poems, stories, directions, nonfiction materials, fairy tales, and folk tales.

- ❏ Begin to identify beginning, middle, and end of a story, with support and in a group.

- ❏ Begin to use word recognition strategies, with support and in a group.

- ❏ Use context clues (for example: pictures and text) while reading and being read to.

- ❏ Use information from what they have learned to develop vocabulary.

Standard 2 – Writing and Speaking

Students write and speak for a variety of purposes and audiences.

- ❏ Share personal narrative through show and tell.

- ❏ Give and receive feedback, with prompting and support, by sharing, writing, and speaking with others.

- ❏ Begin to form letters correctly with the use of manipulatives such as clay or cornmeal.

- ❏ Develop awareness of story elements, such as character, setting, problem, and solution.

Standard 3 – Language Structure

Students write and speak using conventional grammar, usage, sentence structure, punctuation, capitalization, and spelling.

- ❏ Begin to develop awareness of basic modifiers in group writing and when speaking.

- ❏ Use simple sentences to communicate thoughts and ideas when speaking.

- ❏ Differentiate between capital and lower case letters, with support.

- ❏ Use letters to represent words.

Standard 4 – Thinking and Viewing

Students apply thinking skills to their reading, writing, speaking, listening, and viewing.

- ❑ Practice listening skills, with support and in a group, in relation to understanding directions.
- ❑ Begin to use speaking and listening, in a group and with support, to define and solve problems.
- ❑ Begin to respond to oral presentations, in a group and with support, based on personal experience as a listener and speaker.

Standard 5 – Research

Students read to locate, select, and make use of relevant information from a variety of media, reference, and technological sources.

- ❑ Begin to develop appropriate questions, in a group and with support, and identify likely resources.
- ❑ Begin to recognize organizational features of printed text, in a group and with support (for example: title, author, and illustrator).

Standard 6 – Literature and Culture

Students read and recognize literature as a record and expression of cultural heritage.

- ❑ Listen to, respond to, and discuss a variety of literature.
- ❑ Listen to classic literature.
- ❑ Listen to and respond to literature, in a group and with support, related to the heritage of the United States.

KINDERGARTEN

MATH

Standard 1 – Number Sense
Students develop number sense, use numbers and number relationships in problem-solving situations, and communicate the reasoning used in solving these problems.

- ❑ Read, write, compare, and order whole numbers up to 10.
- ❑ Explore strategies for estimation.
- ❑ Compare numbers less than 10 (less than, greater than).
- ❑ Associate numerals up to 10 with sets of objects.

Standard 2 – Patterns and Algebra
Students use algebraic methods to explore, model, and describe patterns and functions involving numbers, shapes, data, and graphs in problem-solving situations and communicate the reasoning used in solving these problems.

- ❑ Recognize and identify number patterns when counting by 2's, 5's, and 10's.
- ❑ Identify, reproduce, extend, create, and describe simple patterns and sequences involving color, shape, size, and rhythm.
- ❑ Correctly place data onto a simple chart or graph.
- ❑ Identify common characteristics of a set of objects.
- ❑ Place objects into appropriate sets according to common characteristics.

Standard 3 – Statistics and Probability
Students use data collection and analysis, statistics, and probability in problem-solving situations and communicate the reasoning used in solving these problems.

- ❑ Represent data using concrete objects.
- ❑ Identify relevant information.
- ❑ Identify more or less on a pictograph.

Boxes of Seeds Sold by Troop 312	
Flower Seeds	🌼 🌼 🌼 🌼
Vegetable Seeds	🥕 🥕 🥕
Herb Seeds	🌿 🌿 🌿
Birdseed	🐦 🐦

KINDERGARTEN

Standard 4 – Geometry

Students use geometric concepts, properties, and relationships in problem-solving situations and communicate the reasoning used in solving these problems.

- ❑ Identify circles, squares, rectangles, triangles, ovals, and diamonds (using familiar everyday objects, manipulatives, or pictures).

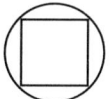

- ❑ Use familiar manipulatives to recognize shapes and their relationships (for example: pasta, boxes, blocks).

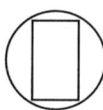

- ❑ Sort objects by size and shape.

- ❑ Recognize shapes of objects familiar to them in their environment (for example: circles, squares, and triangles in classroom, home, and sports).

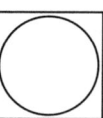

Standard 5 – Measurement

Students use a variety of tools and techniques to measure, apply the results in problem-solving situations, and communicate the reasoning used in solving these problems.

- ❑ Estimate and measure length using nonstandard units (for example: hands, shoes, etc.).

- ❑ Compare and order objects to some attribute (for example: tallest to shortest, biggest to smallest).

- ❑ Demonstrate the process of measuring using a grid path.

- ❑ Without using measuring tools, describe the measures of familiar objects (for example: tall, taller, tallest; older, younger).

- ❑ Count the length of a given path, using the spaces on a grid.

KINDERGARTEN

Standard 6 – Computation
Students link concepts and procedures as they develop and use computational techniques, including estimation, mental arithmetic, paper and pencil, calculators, and computers, in problem-solving situations and communicate the reasoning used in solving these problems.

- ❑ Explore the conceptual meanings for addition and subtraction operations. (For example: If there are 8 boys and 7 girls, how many children are here today? If we have 15 children in the class and 2 are absent, how many children are here today?)

- ❑ Identify numbers from 1 to 20.

- ❑ Develop methods for estimating and computing with whole numbers by using physical models.

- ❑ Be exposed to the many methods that can be used for whole number calculation.

SCIENCE

Standard 1 – Scientific Investigation
Students understand the processes of scientific investigation and design as well as conduct, communicate about, and evaluate such investigations.

- ❑ Explore science in their environment through the use of the five senses.

- ❑ Use simple scientific tools (magnifying glasses, tweezers, etc.).

- ❑ Observe, compare, and describe structures of animals and plants.

- ❑ Communicate observations verbally and by drawing pictures.

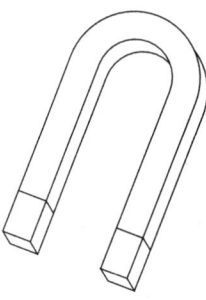

Standard 2 – Physical Science

Students understand common properties, forms, and changes in matter and energy (with a focus on physics and chemistry).

- ❑ Compare objects according to different properties: size, shape, color, etc.
- ❑ Observe the sun's energy (for example: solar calculator, melting snow).
- ❑ Compare energy quantities (for example: hotter and colder).
- ❑ Describe orally or demonstrate the variety of ways that matter (objects or substances) can be put together or changed (for example: clay, paint, paper).

Standard 3 – Life Science

Students understand the characteristics and structure of living things, the processes of life, and how living things interact with each other and their environment (with a focus on biology, anatomy, physiology, botany, zoology, ecology).

- ❑ Observe, compare, and describe properties and parts of plants (root, leaf, stem).
- ❑ Study habitat, structure, and behavior of a variety of animals (fish, snails, worms, bugs).
- ❑ Distinguish between healthy and unhealthy foods.
- ❑ Observe differences in appearance of humans as they grow over time.

Standard 4 – Earth and Space Science

Students understand the processes and interactions of Earth's systems and the structure and dynamics of Earth and other objects in space (with a focus on geology, meteorology, astronomy, oceanography).

Not addressed at this level.

Standard 5 – Science, Technology, and Human Activity

Students understand interrelationships among science, technology, and human activity and how they can affect the world.

- ❏ Name things used in the classroom that are from the earth (for example: water, food, soil).
- ❏ Distinguish between recyclable and throw-away.
- ❏ Identify jobs people do in the school and the tools they use.
- ❏ Identify ways that an individual can take care of the earth.

Standard 6 – Scientific Connections

Students understand that science involves a particular way of knowing and understanding common connections among scientific disciplines.

- ❏ Perform experiments with materials to notice change.
- ❏ Collect data gained from direct experience (for example: pets, dogs, cats, etc.).
- ❏ Compare data collected with other classmates.
- ❏ Characterize different science explorations in which the class participates (for example: studying living vs. nonliving).

GEOGRAPHY

Standard 1 – People, Places, and Environments

Students know how to use and construct maps, globes, and other geographic tools to locate and derive information about people, places, and environments.

- ❏ Recognize the difference between map and globe.
- ❏ Identify land masses and large bodies of water on maps and globes.
- ❏ Locate on a classroom map where different activities take place.

Standard 2 – Regional Characteristics

Students know the physical and human characteristics of places, and use this knowledge to define and study regions and their patterns of change.

- ❑ Tell what is made by people and what is found in nature.
- ❑ Tell what can be found in a park.

Standard 3 – Earth

Students understand how physical processes shape Earth's surface patterns and systems.

- ❑ Describe the weather and how it affects us.
- ❑ Study the seasons and how they affect people, plants, and animals.
- ❑ Observe how water takes on different forms in different weather.

Standard 4 – Economic, Political, Cultural, and Social Processes

Students understand how economic, political, cultural, and social processes interact to shape patterns of human populations, interdependence, cooperation, and conflict.

- ❑ Discuss how family customs or celebrations of holidays are similar or different.
- ❑ Discuss how types of houses, food, clothing, etc., vary around the world.
- ❑ List similarities and differences between life in large cities, small towns, and rural settings, using pictures, literature, and experiences.

Standard 5 – Human Interactions

Students understand the effects of interactions between human and physical systems and the changes in meaning, use, distribution, and importance of resources.

- ❑ Discuss how pollution and litter affect the environment.
- ❑ Find ways to conserve and recycle/reuse/reduce at home and at school.

Standard 6 – Past, Present, and Future
Students apply knowledge of people, places, and environments to understand the past and present and to plan for the future.

Not addressed at this level.

Reading and writing are essential skills of social studies. The social studies curriculum is subdivided into disciplines. For clarity these are listed separately, yet in a kindergarten classroom these will often be taught within a larger thematic unit. This is called integration of subjects.

HISTORY

Standard 1 – Chronological Organization
Students understand the chronological organization of history and how to organize events and people into major eras to identify and explain historical relationships.

- Use a calendar to distinguish between day, week, month, and year.

Standard 2 – Historical Inquiry
Students know how to use the processes and resources of historical inquiry.

- Through literature, compare and contrast life in the past to life in the present.

Standard 3 – Diverse Societies
Students understand that societies are diverse and have changed over time.

- Discuss holidays and celebrations of different families and cultures.

- Find out about different cultures through literature.

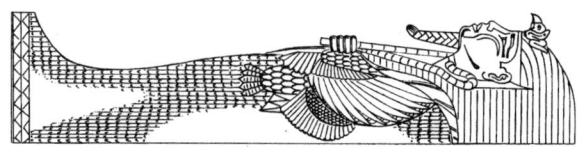

Standard 4 – Science, Technology, and Economic Activity

Students understand how science, technology, and economic activity have developed, changed, and affected societies throughout history.

- ❏ List ways that technology affects their life.

Standard 5 – Political Institutions and Theories

Students understand political institutions and theories that have developed and changed over time.

- ❏ Explain the need for classroom rules.
- ❏ Discuss why we celebrate national holidays: Martin Luther King, Jr. Day, President's Day, Thanksgiving.
- ❏ Learn the Pledge of Allegiance.

Standard 6 – Religion and Philosophy

Students know that religious and philosophical ideas have been powerful forces throughout history.

- ❏ Discuss ways different families celebrate holidays and beliefs of various peoples.

Reading and writing are essential skills of social studies. The social studies curriculum is subdivided into disciplines. For clarity these are listed separately, yet in a kindergarten classroom these will often be taught within a larger thematic unit. This is called integration of subjects.

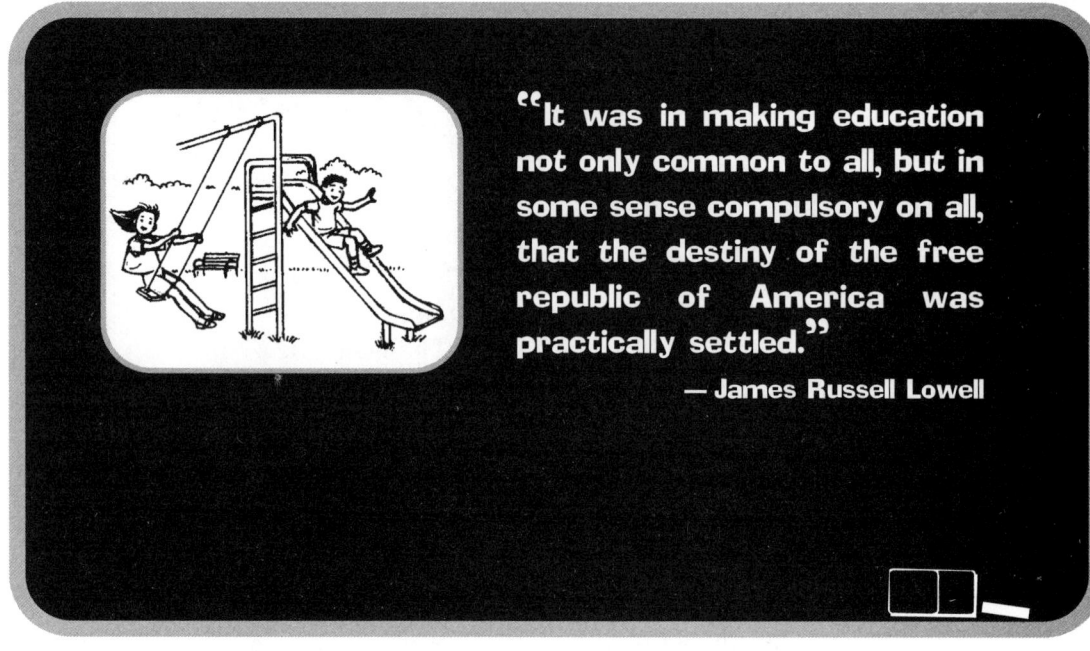

"It was in making education not only common to all, but in some sense compulsory on all, that the destiny of the free republic of America was practically settled."
— James Russell Lowell

First Grade

Language Arts
Math
Science
Geography
History

PARENTS' GUIDE TO STANDARDS

1 FIRST GRADE

 **LANGUAGE ARTS**

Standard 1 – Reading
Students read and understand a variety of materials.

- ❑ Use comparing and contrasting as comprehension strategies.
- ❑ Identify, in a group, what is known and needs to be known about a topic before being read to.
- ❑ Begin to apply word recognition strategies and develop vocabulary, with support, while reading simple text and being read a variety of materials.
- ❑ Begin to develop reading strategies, in a group, for different reading purposes; identify organizational patterns of stories (for example: beginning, middle, and end); and identify different purposes of reading.
- ❑ Begin to use word recognition strategies (including vocabulary and background knowledge, sound-letter relationships/phonics and context clues in pictures and sentence structure).
- ❑ Use information from what they have learned to develop vocabulary.

Standard 2 – Writing and Speaking
Students write and speak for a variety of purposes and audiences.

- ❑ Begin to think of and develop ideas for a variety of writing and speaking purposes (for example: in a group and with support, develop and present a puppet show or flannel board story; at the end of a unit, write a fact or two learned).
- ❑ Share writing and speaking with others.
- ❑ Begin to generate topics for writing and speaking, and to develop and organize ideas for writing and speaking. (Strategies may include brainstorming, peer conferencing, drawing, and webbing.)
- ❑ Begin to write one or more sentences on a topic.
- ❑ Use vocabulary to communicate messages clearly when speaking and with support when writing.
- ❑ Develop awareness of words (for example: introducing students to words with similar vowel sounds).

Standard 3 – Language Structure

Students write and speak using conventional grammar, usage, sentence structure, punctuation, capitalization, and spelling.

- ❏ Develop correct subject-verb agreement when speaking.
- ❏ Begin to use correct capitalization, with support in a group, at the beginning of sentences and with proper nouns.
- ❏ Begin to spell some phonetically regular words using dominant sounds heard.
- ❏ Identify long and short vowels.

Standard 4 – Thinking and Viewing

Students apply thinking skills to their reading, writing, speaking, listening, and viewing.

- ❏ Make predictions and draw conclusions, in a group and with support, about stories when being read to and reading using illustrations, title, and context clues.
- ❏ Begin to formulate questions, in a group with support, about what has been read and what they hear, view, and write.

Standard 5 – Research

Students read to locate, select, and make use of relevant information from a variety of media, reference, and technological sources.

- ❏ Locate appropriate resources, in a group and with support, including books and wall charts.
- ❏ Alphabetize to the first letter as an aid in locating information.
- ❏ Begin to use organizational skills, with support.

Standard 6 – Literature and Culture

Students read and recognize literature as a record and expression of cultural heritage.

- ❏ Listen to and, with support, read, respond to, and discuss a variety of literature.
- ❏ Listen to, respond to, and discuss literature, with support and in a group, as a way to explore similarities and differences among stories from a variety of cultures.

1 FIRST GRADE

 MATH

Standard 1 – Number Sense
Students develop number sense, use numbers and number relationships in problem-solving situations, and communicate the reasoning used in solving these problems.

- ❑ Read, write, compare, and order whole numbers up to 99.
- ❑ Demonstrate one-to-one correspondence using concrete objects.
- ❑ Use manipulatives, a number line, and place value manipulatives to generate different representations for a given number.
- ❑ Tell a story that explains a numerical situation.
- ❑ Understand that order does not affect addition (commutative property of addition).
- ❑ Identify numbers as odd or even; count by 2's, 5's, and 10's.

Standard 2 – Patterns and Algebra
Students use algebraic methods to explore, model, and describe patterns and functions involving numbers, shapes, data, and graphs in problem-solving situations and communicate the reasoning used in solving these problems.

- ❑ Use manipulatives, words, simple tables, graphs, and charts to describe patterns and other relationships.
- ❑ Observe and explain how a change in one quantity can produce a change in another (for example: the relationship between the number of bicycles and the number of wheels).
- ❑ Label sets according to common characteristics (for example: color, size, and shape).
- ❑ Determine a rule that shows how to continue a pattern made of shapes.

Standard 3 – Statistics and Probability
Students use data collection and analysis, statistics, and probability in problem-solving situations and communicate the reasoning used in solving these problems.

- ❑ Record data using pictorial representations.
- ❑ Obtain information and relationships from graphs.
- ❑ Use a bar graph to compare data.

First Grade

Standard 4 – Geometry

Students use geometric concepts, properties, and relationships in problem-solving situations and communicate the reasoning used in solving these problems.

- Sort and classify objects by shape (using familiar everyday objects, manipulatives, or pictures).
- Follow directional diagrams (for example: draw paths on grid squares from one point to another and determine their length).
- Use spatial reasoning to estimate differences in volume and area.

Standard 5 – Measurement

Students use a variety of tools and techniques to measure, apply the results in problem-solving situations, and communicate the reasoning used in solving these problems.

- Estimate and measure length using nonstandard units (for example: steps, strides, etc.).
- Read a clock (hour intervals) and estimate time duration (how much time has passed) using standard and nonstandard units.
- Compare relative perimeter and area using nonstandard units.
- Compare relative temperature (for example: hotter than, colder than).
- Demonstrate the process of measuring length using a grid path and time using a calendar.
- Compare the measures of familiar objects (for example: bigger than, older than, taller than) without using measuring tools.

First Grade

Standard 6 – Computation
Students link concepts and procedures as they develop and use computational techniques, including estimation, mental arithmetic, paper and pencil, calculators, and computers, in problem-solving situations and communicate the reasoning used in solving these problems.

- ❑ Demonstrate conceptual meaning for addition and subtraction operations using whole numbers. (For example: When two sets are combined, a larger set is produced. When a portion of a set is removed, the remaining set is smaller.)
- ❑ Demonstrate proficiency with basic addition facts (1-10).
- ❑ Develop methods to explain estimation with whole numbers when adding.
- ❑ Use various methods for computing whole numbers in problem-solving situations, including mental arithmetic, estimation, paper-and-pencil algorithms, calculator, and other mechanical methods for addition.

 SCIENCE

Standard 1 – Scientific Investigation
Students understand the processes of scientific investigation and design as well as conduct, communicate about, and evaluate such investigations.

- ❑ Communicate observations on calendars and in journals.
- ❑ Follow a plan to conduct an investigation.

Standard 2 — Physical Science
Students understand common properties, forms, and changes in matter and energy (with a focus on physics and chemistry).

- ❑ Identify factors that affect motion (mass, size, texture).
- ❑ Make observations and gather data on quantities associated with energy, movement, and change.
- ❑ Describe interactions that produce changes in a system: balance, stability, mixtures, etc.
- ❑ Observe and compare stable and unstable systems, rotation, spinning, and rolling through the study of balance, stability, and motion.

Standard 3 – Life Science

Students understand the characteristics and structure of living things, the processes of life, and how living things interact with each other and their environment (with a focus on biology, anatomy, physiology, botany, zoology, ecology).

- ❑ Observe and describe the changes that occur as plants grow and develop.
- ❑ Understand living vs. nonliving.
- ❑ Recognize that green plants need energy from sunlight in addition to various raw materials.
- ❑ Recognize the structure of the food pyramid.

Standard 4 – Earth and Space Science

Students understand the processes and interactions of Earth's systems and the structure and dynamics of Earth and other objects in space (with a focus on geology, meteorology, astronomy, oceanography).

- ❑ Identify changes in weather by participating in the decision-making process of dressing appropriately for various weather conditions.
- ❑ Collect and record data on temperature and precipitation.
- ❑ Observe and name three common cloud formations: cirrus, stratus, and cumulus.
- ❑ Compare seasons.

Standard 5 – Science, Technology, and Human Activity

Students understand interrelationships among science, technology, and human activity and how they can affect the world.

- ❑ Identify Earth's resources that first graders use.
- ❑ As a team, invent a device that solves an age-appropriate problem.
- ❑ Relate technology used by parents, friends, and neighbors in their careers.
- ❑ Know that some objects occur in nature, whereas others have been designed and made by people to solve human problems.

First Grade

Standard 6 – Scientific Concepts
Students understand that science involves a particular way of knowing and understanding common connections among scientific disciplines.

- Continue to experiment.
- Collect data gained from direct experience and record on individual charts.
- Recognize that when a scientific experiment is done in the same way in different locations, the experiment generally has the same results.
- Make predictions based upon identified patterns (for example: weather).

GEOGRAPHY

Standard 1 – People, Places, and Environments
Students know how to use and construct maps, globes, and other geographic tools to locate and derive information about people, places, and environments.

- Make and use a map of the classroom.
- Locate places on a school map.
- Trace a route to different places on a school map.
- Locate their town or city on a map of their state.
- Locate their state on a United States map.

Standard 2 – Regional Characteristics
Students know the physical and human characteristics of places, and use this knowledge to define and study regions and their patterns of change.

- Describe how places look between school and home (for example: hilly, flat, river, pond).
- Discuss where humans have changed the earth in local neighborhoods.
- Describe a park, a farm, a city, and a neighborhood.
- Compare and contrast a farm or ranch and a city.

Standard 3 – Earth

Students understand how physical processes shape Earth's surface patterns and systems.

- Observe and describe weather and its effects on the environment.
- Identify Earth's features on maps (for example: rivers, oceans).
- Discuss what happens to Earth in a flood, earthquake, or volcanic eruption.
- Identify local physical features (for example: hills, drainage ditch).

Standard 4 – Economic, Political, Cultural, and Social Processes

Students understand how economic, political, cultural, and social processes interact to shape patterns of human populations, interdependence, cooperation, and conflict.

- Discuss the reason people come to school in different ways (for example: walk, bus, car).
- Identify elements of culture (for example: food, dress, traditions, education, family, religion, music, and arts).
- Introduce a map to locate where traditions have come from.
- Identify places to acquire basic goods and services.
- Discuss reasons why people might settle in rural or urban settings (using literature).
- Discuss and list why there are boundaries on the school playground.

Standard 5 – Human Interactions

Students understand the effects of interactions between human and physical systems and the changes in meaning, use, distribution, and importance of resources.

- Identify the impact of human activity on different areas of the playground.
- Continue to discuss ways people deal with natural environment (for example: weather, pollution, and litter).
- Discuss how recreational activities are done in places due to physical environment (for example: skiing, sledding, boating, hiking).
- Classify activities as recycle, reuse, or reduce.

FIRST GRADE

Standard 6 – Past, Present, and Future

Students apply knowledge of people, places, and environments to understand the past and present and to plan for the future.

- ❑ Read literature about children and families living in the past.

Reading and writing are essential skills of social studies. The social studies curriculum is subdivided into disciplines. For clarity these are listed separately, yet in a first-grade classroom these will often be taught within a larger thematic unit. This is called integration of subjects.

 HISTORY

Standard 1 – Chronological Organization

Students understand the chronological organization of history and how to organize events and people into major eras to identify and explain historical relationships.

- ❑ Differentiate broad categories of historical time (for example: long ago, yesterday, today, tomorrow).
- ❑ Sequence events in literature and construct a time line.

Standard 2 – Historical Inquiry

Students know how to use the processes and resources of historical inquiry.

- ❑ Pose questions about the past—begin to pose questions about their own lives and their own family history.
- ❑ Recognize how writing, photographs, and graphs show events in the past.
- ❑ Identify when a story takes place (past, present, future).
- ❑ Identify how Native Americans kept their history.

Standard 3 – Diverse Societies

Students understand that societies are diverse and have changed over time.

- ❑ Discuss how the presence and contributions of Native Americans have affected our lives.
- ❑ Identify roles of family members.
- ❑ Use literature to learn about cultures around the world.

First Grade

Standard 4 – Science, Technology, and Economic Activity

Students understand how science, technology, and economic activity have developed, changed, and affected societies throughout history.

- ❏ Identify scientific and technological developments that affect their family or school environment (for example: computers, copy machines, telephones, televisions, cars).
- ❏ Give examples of different ways to allocate resources.
- ❏ Count money.

Standard 5 – Political Institutions and Theories

Students understand political institutions and theories that have developed and changed over time.

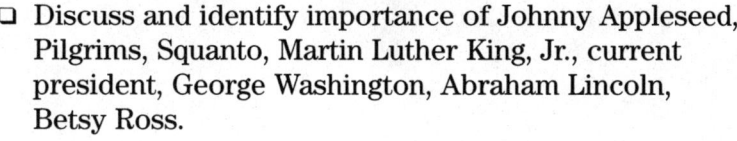

- ❏ Using literature, examine different kinds of leaders (for example: king, dictator, president, mayor, governor).
- ❏ Discuss and identify importance of Johnny Appleseed, Pilgrims, Squanto, Martin Luther King, Jr., current president, George Washington, Abraham Lincoln, Betsy Ross.
- ❏ Discuss and identify importance and historical context of Pledge of Allegiance, Columbus Day, Thanksgiving, Martin Luther King, Jr. Day, Valentine's Day, Earth Day, Independence Day, American flag, eagle.
- ❏ Discuss how various groups have gained or lost political freedom.

Standard 6 – Religion and Philosophy

Students know that religious and philosophical ideas have been powerful forces throughout history.

- ❏ Identify traditions in their families.
- ❏ Read and listen to literature, including multicultural works, folk tales, and ballads.
- ❏ Participate in various forms of expression (for example: folk dances, songs, games, visual arts).

Reading and writing are essential skills of social studies. The social studies curriculum is subdivided into disciplines. For clarity these are listed separately, yet in a first-grade classroom these will often be taught within a larger thematic unit. This is called integration of subjects.

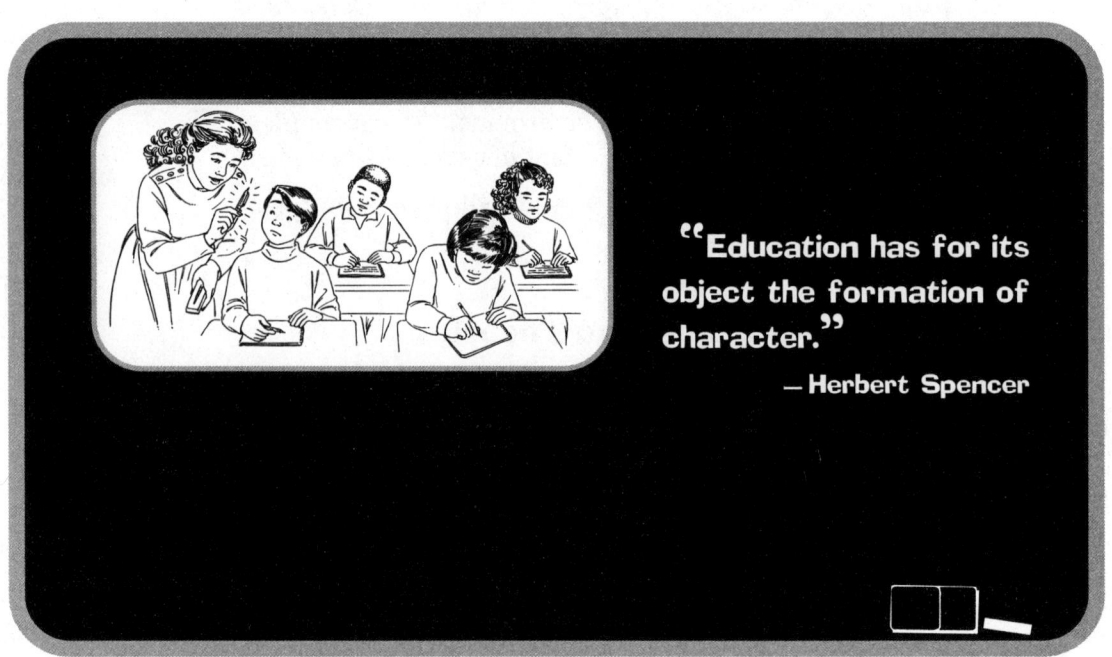

Second Grade

Language Arts
Math
Science
Geography
History

Parents' Guide to Standards

SECOND GRADE

LANGUAGE ARTS

Standard 1 – Reading
Students read and understand a variety of materials.

- ❏ Use sound-letter relationships and phonics as word recognition strategies.
- ❏ Identify what they already know and need to know, in a group, about a topic before they read about it.
- ❏ Apply word recognition strategies when reading a variety of materials: rhymes and poems, stories, directions, nonfiction material, fairy tales and folk tales, including those from other communities and cultures.
- ❏ Use information from reading to enhance vocabulary.
- ❏ Use information from what they have learned to develop vocabulary.

Standard 2 – Writing and Speaking
Students write and speak for a variety of purposes and audiences.

- ❏ Begin to adapt word choice, with support, to various audiences.
- ❏ Give and receive feedback, with prompting and support, as an aid in beginning to edit, revise, and produce a finished product in speech and writing for an audience beyond the classroom.
- ❏ Use story parts (beginning, middle, and end).
- ❏ Begin using descriptive vocabulary and, with support, begin to use figures of speech to communicate a clear message.
- ❏ Develop awareness of nouns, verbs, and homonyms.

Standard 3 – Language Structure
Students write and speak using conventional grammar, usage, sentence structure, punctuation, capitalization, and spelling.

- ❏ Use correct subject-verb agreement when writing, with support.
- ❏ Explore using compound sentences when writing in a group.
- ❏ Begin to use correct basic capitalization and basic ending punctuation of simple sentences.
- ❏ Correctly spell frequently used words.

Second Grade

Standard 4 – Thinking and Viewing

Students apply thinking skills to their reading, writing, speaking, listening, and viewing.

- Use reading, writing, speaking, and listening, with support, to define and solve problems.
- Begin to differentiate between fact and opinion, with support, in written and spoken forms.
- Begin to recognize author's point of view, in a group and with support.

Standard 5 – Research

Students read to locate, select, and make use of relevant information from a variety of media, reference, and technological sources.

- Recognize organizational features of printed text (for example: title, author, illustrator, title page, page numbering, table of contents, structure of text, index, chapter headings, copyright information, alphabetizing) and some features of electronic media.
- Begin to sort information, with support, as it relates to a specific topic or purpose.
- Begin to give credit for borrowed information, with support, by telling or listing sources (for example: book title and author).

Standard 6 – Literature and Culture

Students read and recognize literature as a record and expression of cultural heritage.

- Use literary terminology (for example: character, setting, problem, solution).
- Read, respond to, and discuss a variety of literature (for example: fiction, rhymes and poems, nonfiction).
- Begin to read, respond to, and discuss content area material, with support.

SECOND GRADE

MATH

Standard 1 – Number Sense
Students develop number sense, use numbers and number relationships in problem-solving situations, and communicate the reasoning used in solving these problems.

- ❏ Demonstrate one-to-one correspondence using concrete objects.
- ❏ Generate different representations for a given number.
- ❏ Identify and name common unit fractions.
- ❏ Use place value manipulatives to represent decimal numbers and represent money as decimal numerals.
- ❏ Use place value manipulatives to demonstrate ones, tens, and hundreds place for numbers 0 to 999.
- ❏ Read, name, count, and order time in intervals of minutes, hours, days, months, and years.

Standard 2 – Patterns and Algebra
Students use algebraic methods to explore, model, and describe patterns and functions involving numbers, shapes, data, and graphs in problem-solving situations and communicate the reasoning used in solving these problems.

- ❏ Identify, reproduce, extend, create, and describe more complex patterns and sequences involving color, shape, size, and number.
- ❏ Construct, use, and interpret simple tables, graphs, and charts to describe relationships and solve problems.
- ❏ Use >, <, and = to compare two sets of numbers.
- ❏ Determine a rule that describes the generation of a sequence of shapes and numbers.

Second Grade

Standard 3 – Statistics and Probability

Students use data collection and analysis, statistics, and probability in problem-solving situations and communicate the reasoning used in solving these problems.

- ❏ Collect data; place information on a graph with labeled axis.
- ❏ Obtain information from bar graphs.
- ❏ Given data displayed in different kinds of graphs, determine greatest and least, greater than and less than.
- ❏ Generate data from random events.
- ❏ Use the concept of chance to determine possible outcomes.

Standard 4 – Geometry

Students use geometric concepts, properties, and relationships in problem-solving situations and communicate the reasoning used in solving these problems.

- ❏ Classify various two-dimensional geometric shapes according to given attributes (using everyday objects, manipulatives, or pictures).

Standard 5 – Measurement

Students use a variety of tools and techniques to measure, apply the results in problem-solving situations, and communicate the reasoning used in solving these problems.

- ❏ Estimate and measure length (whole inch and whole centimeter) and hour (hour and half-hour intervals).
- ❏ Demonstrate the process of measuring length, time, and money, given the appropriate tools.
- ❏ Without using tools, describe and compare the measure of familiar objects (for example: heights of friends, weights of books, inside vs. outside temperatures).
- ❏ Use geometric figures to demonstrate the terms "greater than" and "less than" as they relate to measurement and number sense.
- ❏ Correctly identify and classify shapes within their environment.

SECOND GRADE

Standard 6 – Computation

Students link concepts and procedures as they develop and use computational techniques, including estimation, mental arithmetic, paper and pencil, calculators, and computers, in problem-solving situations and communicate the reasoning used in solving these problems.

- ❑ Demonstrate conceptual meaning for addition and subtraction operations using whole numbers (for example: when two sets are combined, a larger set is produced; when a portion of a set is removed, the remaining set is smaller).

- ❑ Demonstrate the conceptual meaning of fractions, using a physical model, with the ability to apply the fraction $\frac{1}{2}$ to a problem-solving situation.

- ❑ Demonstrate conceptual meaning and proficiency with basic addition and subtraction facts (for example: 2 digit without regrouping).

- ❑ Develop methods to explain estimation with whole numbers when adding and subtracting (all basic facts).

SCIENCE

Standard 1 – Scientific Investigation

Students understand the processes of scientific investigation and design as well as conduct, communicate about, and evaluate such investigations.

- ❑ As a class, ask questions and state predictions (hypotheses) that can be addressed through scientific investigation (scientific method).

- ❑ As a class, determine variables and controls.

- ❑ As a class, select and use the tools necessary to solve the problem.

- ❑ As a class, observe and give a reasonable explanation for data collected.

Second Grade

Standard 2 – Physical Science

Students understand common properties, forms, and changes in matter and energy (with a focus on physics and chemistry).

- Know that objects can be described and classified by their composition and physical properties.
- Explore properties of liquids and solids.

Standard 3 – Life Science

Students understand the characteristics and structure of living things, the processes of life, and how living things interact with each other and their environment (with a focus on biology, anatomy, physiology, botany, zoology, ecology).

- Observe and compare the needs, structure, behavior, and life cycles of a variety of insects: milkweed bugs, butterflies, silkworms.
- Compare the lifestyles of various insects: habitats, place in the food chain, who eats them, whom they eat.
- Identify characteristics common to vertebrates.
- Know that there is variation among individuals within a population.

Standard 4 – Earth and Space Science

Students understand the processes and interactions of Earth's systems and the structure and dynamics of Earth and other objects in space (with a focus on geology, meteorology, astronomy, oceanography).

- Identify uses of rocks and soils.
- Recognize that fossils are evidence of past life.
- Know that Earth materials consist of solid rocks, soils, liquid water, and the gases of the atmosphere.
- Investigate properties of clay and soil.

SECOND GRADE

Standard 5 – Science, Technology, and Human Activity
Students understand interrelationships among science, technology, and human activity and how they can affect the world.

- ❑ Recognize renewable and nonrenewable Earth resources.
- ❑ Describe a resource-related community activity in which they can participate.
- ❑ Describe technology used for careers in the community.
- ❑ Identify activities that benefit the community in which students can participate.

Standard 6 – Scientific Connections
Students understand that science involves a particular way of knowing and understanding common connections among scientific disciplines.

- ❑ Continue to collect data gained from direct experience and record on individual charts.
- ❑ Recognize that systems involve both living and nonliving things.
- ❑ Organize and classify scientific information (gain an awareness of various science disciplines).
- ❑ Understand that it is helpful to work with a team in science and to share findings with others.

GEOGRAPHY

Standard 1 – People, Places, and Environments
Students know how to use and construct maps, globes, and other geographic tools to locate and derive information about people, places, and environments.

- ❑ Understand different uses of world, U.S., state, and community maps.
- ❑ Use a globe to locate continents and oceans.
- ❑ Apply directions of north/south/east/west to the school building.
- ❑ Identify industrial, commercial, residential, rural, and recreational areas of the community.

Second Grade

Standard 2 – Regional Characteristics
Students know the physical and human characteristics of places, and use this knowledge to define and study regions and their patterns of change.

- ❏ Compare and contrast rural life and city life.
- ❏ Develop awareness of different uses for areas (for example: parks).

Standard 3 – Earth
Students understand how physical processes shape Earth's surface patterns and systems.

- ❏ Describe the water cycle.
- ❏ Observe the seasons.
- ❏ Observe the length of daylight during the seasons.
- ❏ Gain awareness of the calendar and seasons.
- ❏ Identify local birds and common animals.

Standard 4 – Economic, Political, Cultural, and Social Processes
Students understand how economic, political, cultural, and social processes interact to shape patterns of human populations, interdependence, cooperation, and conflict.

- ❏ Give reasons why people came to the local community in the beginning.
- ❏ Describe the past and present forms of communication and transportation used in the local community.
- ❏ Describe how local communities work together and deal with conflict.

Standard 5 – Human Interactions
Students understand the effects of interactions between human and physical systems and the changes in meaning, use, distribution, and importance of resources.

- ❏ Discuss local community growth.
- ❏ List some natural resources and give examples of what can be recycled.

Second Grade

Standard 6 – Past, Present, and Future
Students apply knowledge of people, places, and environments to understand the past and present and to plan for the future.

- ❑ Make a time line, as a class or individuals, of local community history.
- ❑ Read literature about children living in the past.

Reading and writing are essential skills of social studies. The social studies curriculum is subdivided into disciplines. For clarity these are listed separately, yet in a second-grade classroom these will often be taught within a larger thematic unit. This is called integration of subjects.

History

Standard 1 – Chronological Organization
Students understand the chronological organization of history and know how to organize events and people into major eras to identify and explain historical relationships.

- ❑ Distinguish between past, present, and future time in the community.
- ❑ Begin to construct a brief oral narrative describing, in sequence, a past event.

Standard 2 – Historical Inquiry
Students know how to use the processes and resources of historical inquiry.

- ❑ Pose questions about the history of the community.
- ❑ Identify the main idea of historical stories.
- ❑ Identify where historical information came from.
- ❑ Begin to make connections between the past and present in their local community's history.

SECOND GRADE

Standard 3 – Diverse Societies
Students understand that societies are diverse and have changed over time.

- ❏ Identify cultural heritage evident in their community.
- ❏ Explain the cultural origins of place (for example: names in the community).

Standard 4 – Science, Technology, and Economic Activity
Students understand how science, technology, and economic activity have developed, changed, and affected societies throughout history.

- ❏ Describe economic needs and wants of a community (for example: education, recreation, transportation, city services).

Standard 5 – Political Institutions and Theories
Students understand political institutions and theories that have developed and changed over time.

- ❏ Give examples of various ways decisions are made: majority vote, compromise, etc.
- ❏ Describe the people who make decisions in the city government.

Standard 6 – Religion and Philosophy
Students know that religious and philosophical ideas have been powerful forces throughout history.

- ❏ Recite the Pledge of Allegiance and recognize it as a statement of our country's foundation.
- ❏ Read and listen to history, daily life, and beliefs of people who settled in their local community.

Reading and writing are essential skills of social studies. The social studies curriculum is subdivided into disciplines. For clarity these are listed separately, yet in a second-grade classroom these will often be taught within a larger thematic unit. This is called integration of subjects.

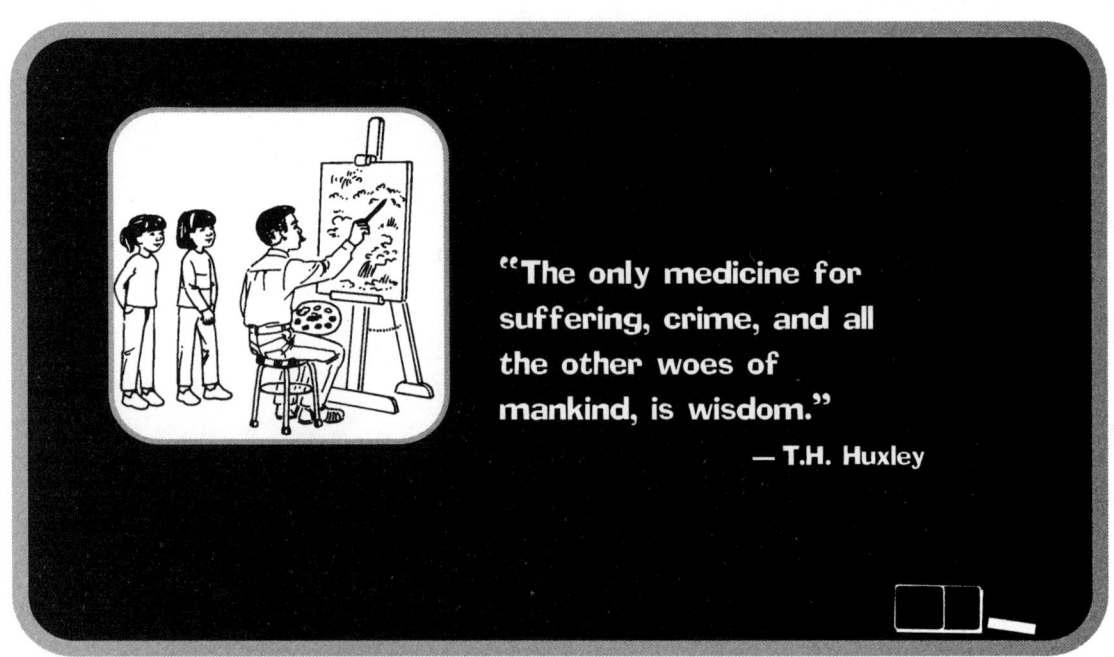

THIRD GRADE

Language Arts
Math
Science
Geography
History

PARENTS' GUIDE TO STANDARDS

THIRD GRADE

LANGUAGE ARTS

Standard 1 – Reading

Students read and understand a variety of materials.

- Use sound-letter relationships and phonics as word recognition strategies.
- Make connections between the reading and what is already known through experiences such as group discussions and journal writing.
- Use comprehension strategies, with support (including comparing/contrasting, developing awareness of text structure, identifying author's purpose or main idea, inferring, predicting, previewing, summarizing, recognizing the use of figures of speech, re-reading, and researching new material).
- Select appropriate reading materials based on interest and readability.
- Continue to develop reading fluency and self-correct reading errors.
- Use information from what they have learned to develop vocabulary.

Standard 2 – Writing and Speaking

Students write and speak for a variety of purposes and audiences.

- Draft, revise, edit, and proofread their own writing, with prompting and support.
- Sequence events appropriately.
- Continue to develop awareness of homonyms, antonyms, and synonyms.
- Write in cursive style.
- Begin to use the computer for word processing.

Standard 3 – Language Structure

Students write and speak using conventional grammar, usage, sentence structure, punctuation, capitalization, and spelling.

- Use modifiers in writing and speaking.
- Use simple sentences and, with support, compound sentences in writing and speaking.
- Begin to use some basic internal punctuation.

- Begin to use abbreviations.
- Use resources to obtain correct spelling (for example: books, word banks, charts, dictionaries).
- Use root words, prefixes, and suffixes.

Standard 4 – Thinking and Viewing

Students apply thinking skills to their reading, writing, speaking, listening, and viewing.

- Begin to predict and draw conclusions about stories using illustrations, title, context, captions, chapter headings.
- Begin to formulate questions about what they read, write, hear, and view.
- Begin to recognize author's point of view.

Standard 5 – Research

Students read to locate, select, and make use of relevant information from a variety of media, reference, and technological sources.

- Locate appropriate resources, in a group (for example: encyclopedias, atlases, nonfiction books, and electronic media).
- Alphabetize to the third letter as an aid in locating information.
- Begin to use organizational skills (for example: highlighting main ideas).

Standard 6 – Literature and Culture

Students read and recognize literature as a record and expression of cultural heritage.

- Use literary terminology (for example: character, setting, problem, solution) and begin to use plot.
- Begin to use new vocabulary from literature in other contexts.
- Listen to and read some classic literature and begin to recognize concept of classic or enduring literature.
- Begin to read, respond to, and discuss, in a group and with support, literature related to the heritage of the United States.

Third Grade

 **Math**

Standard 1 – Number Sense
Students develop number sense, use numbers and number relationships in problem-solving situations, and communicate the reasoning used in solving these problems.

- ❑ Represent a given number with place value manipulatives (including decimals and negatives).
- ❑ Represent decimals as fractions and fractions as decimals by using money.
- ❑ Read, write, order, and compare numerals 0 to 9,999, including decimals and fractions.
- ❑ Use estimation for mental arithmetic in addition and subtraction.

Standard 2 – Patterns and Algebra
Students use algebraic methods to explore, model, and describe patterns and functions involving numbers, shapes, data, and graphs in problem-solving situations and communicate the reasoning used in solving these problems.

- ❑ Identify, reproduce, extend, create, and describe simple patterns and sequences involving whole numbers, negative numbers, fractions, and decimals.
- ❑ Construct, use, and interpret tables, graphs, and charts to describe relationships and solve problems.
- ❑ Use the concept that subtraction is the inverse of addition to solve problems.

Standard 3 – Statistics and Probability
Students use data collection and analysis, statistics, and probability in problem-solving situations and communicate the reasoning used in solving these problems.

- ❑ Construct, read, and interpret displays of data including tables, charts, pictographs, and bar graphs.
- ❑ Given a range of numbers, order the numbers and identify the middle of the range and the number that occurs most often.
- ❑ Find the average (mean) of two numbers using concrete representations.

THIRD GRADE 3

Standard 4 – Geometry

Students use geometric concepts, properties, and relationships in problem-solving situations and communicate the reasoning used in solving these problems.

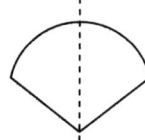

- ❑ Identify, compare, and determine the perimeter and areas of shapes on a grid.
- ❑ Identify, sort, and classify solid geometric shapes (cones, spheres, cylinders, and cubes).
- ❑ Identify shapes that have a line of symmetry.
- ❑ Identify circular, triangular, square, and rectangular objects and recreate their shapes.

Standard 5 – Measurement

Students use a variety of tools and techniques to measure, apply the results in problem-solving situations, and communicate the reasoning used in solving these problems.

- ❑ Estimate and measure length, perimeter, time (5 minute intervals), and capacity (pints, cups, quarts, and gallons) using standard units, with an understanding of the results.
- ❑ Demonstrate the process of measuring length, time, temperature, and money in a given situation.

Standard 6 – Computation

Students link concepts and procedures as they develop and use computational techniques, including estimation, mental arithmetic, paper and pencil, calculators, and computers, in problem-solving situations and communicate the reasoning used in solving these problems.

- ❑ Demonstrate conceptual meanings for addition, subtraction, and multiplication operations using whole numbers.
- ❑ Demonstrate conceptual meaning and proficiency with basic facts for addition, subtraction (2 digit with regrouping), and multiplication (1 digit by 1 digit).
- ❑ Develop methods to explain estimation procedures for adding and subtracting whole numbers with regrouping and multiplying using all basic facts (1-10).
- ❑ Select and use appropriate methods for computing with whole numbers in problem-solving situations from among mental arithmetic, estimation, paper-and-pencil algorithms, and calculator or other mechanical methods in addition, subtraction, and multiplication.

THIRD GRADE

SCIENCE

Standard 1 – Scientific Investigation
Students understand the processes of scientific investigation and design as well as conduct, communicate about, and evaluate such investigations.

- ❑ Ask questions and state predictions (hypotheses), in small groups, that can be addressed through scientific investigation (scientific method).
- ❑ Observe and give a reasonable explanation for data collected, while in small groups.
- ❑ Use tables, pictures, and charts to explain in written form.
- ❑ Organize observations through writing, drawing, and graphing.

Standard 2 – Physical Science
Students understand common properties, forms, and changes in matter and energy (with a focus on physics and chemistry).

- ❑ Separate simple liquid mixtures with simple compositions (for example: oil and water).
- ❑ Investigate nature of sound and vibration.
- ❑ Explore mechanical energy.
- ❑ Observe how sound is created in different musical instruments.

Standard 3 – Life Science
Students understand the characteristics and structure of living things, the processes of life, and how living things interact with each other and their environment (with a focus on biology, anatomy, physiology, botany, zoology, ecology).

- ❑ Investigate basic needs for plants and animals.
- ❑ Investigate invertebrates' interaction with each other and with nonliving parts of their habitat.
- ❑ Draw and describe food chains.

Third Grade

Standard 4 – Earth and Space Science

Students understand the processes and interactions of Earth's systems and the structure and dynamics of Earth and other objects in space (with a focus on geology, meteorology, astronomy, oceanography).

- ❑ Explore properties of water through experimentation (evaporation and condensation).
- ❑ Illustrate how water cycles in nature.
- ❑ Understand phases of moon, eclipse, and differences between stars and planets.
- ❑ Explore how Earth's position affects seasonal changes in different parts of the world.
- ❑ Identify basic components of our solar system.
- ❑ Describe the motion of Earth in relation to the sun (day, night, and year).

Standard 5 – Science, Technology, and Human Activity

Students understand interrelationships among science, technology, and human activity and how they can affect the world.

- ❑ Recognize diversity of resources from all over the world.
- ❑ Describe a worldwide resource-related activity in which students can participate.
- ❑ Investigate technology used in various countries and cultures of the world.
- ❑ Categorize items into groups of natural objects and designed objects.

Standard 6 – Scientific Connections

Students understand that science involves a particular way of knowing and understanding common connections among scientific disciplines.

- ❑ Describe and compare the components and interrelationships of a simple system.
- ❑ Repeat science experiments to see if the same results occur.
- ❑ Compare knowledge gained from direct experience to knowledge gained indirectly (for example: collecting data about student heights and comparing the results to similar data collected in another class or school).
- ❑ Compare a model to what it represents.

THIRD GRADE

GEOGRAPHY

Standard 1 – People, Places, and Environments
Students know how to use and construct maps, globes, and other geographic tools to locate and derive information about people, places, and environments.

- Name cardinal and intermediate (medial) directions: N, S, E, W, NE, NW, SE, SW.
- Identify latitude and longitude on a globe, and use these to identify a specific location.
- Identify legend, key, symbol, and use map keys to identify important places.
- Place continents on globe for spatial relationships.
- Identify seven continents and four oceans on a world map, and identify major geographic features on each continent.
- Identify hemispheres, equator, and prime meridian on maps and globes.

Standard 2 – Regional Characteristics
Students know the physical and human characteristics of places, and use this knowledge to define and study regions and their patterns of change.

- Discuss effects of people (exploration, colonization, industrialization, and urbanization) on the environment (for example: mountains, grasslands, rain forests, deserts).
- Compare and contrast regions found throughout the world.

THIRD GRADE 3

...and how physical processes shape Earth's
...and systems.

...explain how plants and animals adapted to
...environments (for example: rain forests,
...tains, polar regions, grasslands, oceans).

...mosphere of Earth.

...'s axis tilt for summer/winter and
...ution in space.

...egions, desert regions, and polar regions.

...noes, continental drift, and erosion.

...ater cycle, food chain, and life cycle.

...escribe weather differences in each area.

...atural features and systems: land erosion,
...eninsulas, islands, tornadoes, hurricanes,
...rns, water, lakes, oceans, rivers.

...ts and animals in different climate regions
...(for example: rain forests, deserts,
...olar regions, plains, grasslands, oceans).

...litical, Cultural, and Social Processes

...tand how economic, political, cultural, and social
...ct to shape patterns of human populations,
..., cooperation, and conflict.

...te, land formations, and vegetation and
...ect the population distribution in the world.

...people live where they do and why they
...oasts and rivers first and then move inland.

...r map keys to compare and contrast
...nes, industry, literature, food, crops,
...thing, music, jobs, schools, art, family.

...communication and transportation in the
...nity, and compare and contrast with other
...world.

- ❑ Identify factors of settlement and transportation: water, land for crops, safety, space, trees/wood, game for food.

- ❑ Discuss conflict, cooperation, and peaceful relationships between countries and/or states.

THIRD GRADE

Standard 5 – Human Interactions
Students understand the effects of interactions between human and physical systems and the changes in meaning, use, distribution, and importance of resources.

- List advantages and disadvantages of modern technology on the environment.
- Map resource distribution throughout the world.

Standard 6 – Past, Present, and Future
Students apply knowledge of people, places, and environments to understand the past and present and to plan for the future.

- Use maps, pictures, and resources to research how places have changed over time.
- Read stories about native peoples and contrast to how people live today in various parts of the world.
- Describe how volcanoes, continental drift, and earthquakes have changed the earth's surface.

Reading and writing are essential skills of social studies. The social studies curriculum is subdivided into disciplines. For clarity these are listed separately, yet in a third-grade classroom these will often be taught within a larger thematic unit. This is called integration of subjects.

HISTORY

Standard 1 – Chronological Organization
Students understand the chronological organization of history and know how to organize events and people into major eras to identify and explain historical relationships.

- Create simple time lines of historical events.
- Write a narrative that chronologically organizes people or events in their family or school.

THIRD GRADE

Standard 2 – Historical Inquiry
Students know how to use the processes and resources of historical inquiry.

- ❏ Pose questions about the history of a community as it relates to the 7 continents.
- ❏ Gather information about the past from fiction and nonfiction books, oral histories, photography, newspapers, and art works as it relates to the 7 continents.
- ❏ Identify the main ideas of a historical resource.
- ❏ Identify different cultural records as they relate to the 7 continents.
- ❏ Compare past and present-day traditions and events of cultures around the world.

Standard 3 – Diverse Societies
Students understand that societies are diverse and have changed over time.

- ❏ Identify ways that people from all continents have contributed to our state and community.
- ❏ Compare and contrast life in communities around the world.

Standard 4 – Science, Technology, and Economic Activity
Students understand how science, technology, and economic activity have developed, changed, and affected societies throughout history.

- ❏ Describe the impact of irrigation, transportation, and communication on various regions around the world.
- ❏ Identify individual achievements of scientists and inventors from many cultures.
- ❏ Identify movement factors to and from a community based on natural resources and economic wants and needs.
- ❏ Give examples of different ways that decisions are made about natural resources in different cultures.
- ❏ Give examples of systems of exchange in different cultures around the globe.

THIRD GRADE

Standard 5 – Political Institutions and Theories

Students understand political institutions and theories that have developed and changed over time.

- ❏ Explain why cities and towns have laws to maintain order and protect citizens.
- ❏ Give examples of different heads of government around the world.
- ❏ Discuss the exchange of power in the history of various communities around the world.

Standard 6 – Religion and Philosophy

Students know that religious and philosophical ideas have been powerful forces throughout history.

- ❏ Give examples of how the beliefs of people are reflected in the celebrations and practices of their community.
- ❏ Discuss ways that communities depict their history, daily life, and beliefs.

Reading and writing are essential skills of social studies. The social studies curriculum is subdivided into disciplines. For clarity these are listed separately, yet in a third-grade classroom these will often be taught within a larger thematic unit. This is called integration of subjects.

Fourth Grade

Language Arts
Math
Science
Geography
History

Parents' Guide to Standards

4 Fourth Grade

 **LANGUAGE ARTS**

Standard 1 – Reading
Students read and understand a variety of materials.

- ❑ Begin to adjust reading strategies, with support, for different purposes.
- ❑ Apply word recognition strategies when reading a variety of materials: rhymes and poems, stories, directions, nonfiction material, fairy tales, and folk tales, including those from other communities and cultures.
- ❑ Use homophones correctly.
- ❑ Begin to use word origins.
- ❑ Use information from what they have learned to develop vocabulary.

Standard 2 – Writing and Speaking
Students write and speak for a variety of purposes (expository, persuasive, narrative, and creative writing) and audiences.

- ❑ Think of and develop ideas, in a group, for a variety of writing and speaking purposes. For example:
  - Publish a class newsletter or a personal story in a variety of genres.
  - Write a letter to an adult (business or friendly letter) or pen pal.
  - Write or orally present a book report.
- ❑ Share finished pieces.
- ❑ Use character, setting, and plot sequence events appropriately.
- ❑ Begin to write paragraphs, in a group and with support.
- ❑ Use vocabulary, figures of speech, and story elements to communicate messages clearly and precisely.
- ❑ Develop awareness of homonyms, synonyms, and antonyms.
- ❑ Present a final product in publishable form.

Fourth Grade

Standard 3 – Language Structure

Students write and speak using conventional grammar, usage, sentence structure, punctuation, capitalization, and spelling.

- ❏ Identify some parts of speech, such as nouns, verbs, and adjectives.
- ❏ Use simple and compound sentences in writing and speaking.
- ❏ Develop awareness of homophones.

Standard 4 – Thinking and Viewing

Students apply thinking skills to their reading, writing, speaking, listening, and viewing.

- ❏ Practice listening skills in relation to understanding directions of increasing number, length, and complexity.
- ❏ Formulate questions about what they read, write, hear, and view.

Standard 5 – Research

Students read to locate, select, and make use of relevant information from a variety of media, reference, and technological sources.

- ❏ Use organizational features to locate media or electronic information (for example: passwords, entry menu features, pull-down menus, icons, keyword searches).
- ❏ Sort information as it relates to a specific topic or purpose.
- ❏ Give credit for borrowed information by telling or listing sources, including title of book, author, copyright date, and publisher.
- ❏ Use information from research, in a group and with support, to create an end product (written, oral, or visual).

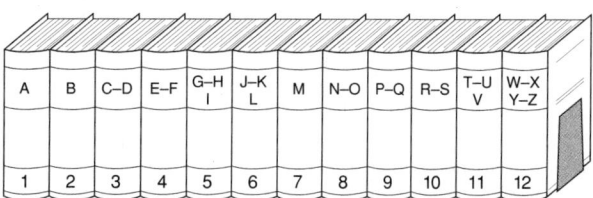

FOURTH GRADE

Standard 6 – Literature and Culture
Students read and recognize literature as a record and expression of cultural heritage.

- ❏ Read, respond to, and discuss a variety of literature (for example: folk tales, legends, myths, fiction, rhymes and poems, nonfiction, and content-area reading).

- ❏ Read, respond to, and discuss literature as a way to explore similarities and differences among stories and the ways in which those stories reflect the ethnic background of the author and the culture in which they were written.

MATH

Standard 1 – Number Sense
Students develop number sense, use numbers and number relationships in problem-solving situations, and communicate the reasoning used in solving these problems.

- ❏ Demonstrate meanings for whole numbers, integers, commonly used fractions, and decimals (for example: money) and represent equivalent forms of the same number through the use of physical models, drawings, calculators, and computers.

- ❏ Read, write, order, and compare whole numbers, integers, unit fractions (e.g. $\frac{1}{4}$, $\frac{1}{5}$) with unlike denominators, and decimals to hundredths as they relate to money.

- ❏ Use number sense to estimate and justify solutions with whole numbers and commonly used fractions.

- ❏ Use numbers in various ways to count, to measure, to label and to indicate location (odd, even, negative, decimals, and fractions) on a number line.

FOURTH GRADE 4

Standard 2 – Patterns and Algebra

Students use algebraic methods to explore, model, and describe patterns and functions involving numbers, shapes, data, and graphs in problem-solving situations and communicate the reasoning used in solving these problems.

- ❏ Identify, reproduce, extend, create, and describe more complex patterns and sequences involving whole numbers, negative numbers, fractions, and decimals.

- ❏ Use tables, graphs, open sentences (n + 5 = 12), and relational diagrams to describe patterns and other relationships (bar, circle, and broken line graphs).

- ❏ Recognize when a pattern or sequence exists and use that information to solve a problem (for example: multiplication is repeated addition and division is repeated subtraction).

Standard 3 – Statistics and Probability

Students use data collection and analysis, statistics, and probability in problem-solving situations and communicate the reasoning used in solving these problems.

- ❏ Read, interpret, and construct simple displays of data, including tables, charts, pictographs, different scales, and bar graphs with an interval of one.

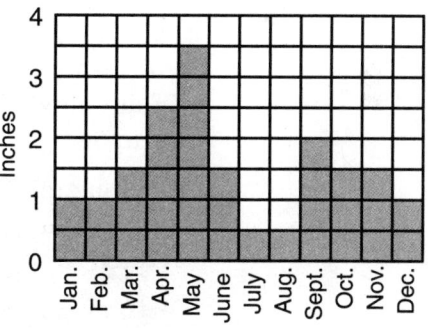

- ❏ Calculate and explain the average (mean) of more than two 2-digit numbers that divide evenly.

- ❏ Generate, analyze, and make predictions based on data (with one variable) obtained from surveys and chance devices (for example: spinners and dice).

- ❏ Demonstrate that predictions can be wrong due to randomness.

Fourth Grade

Standard 4 – Geometry

Students use geometric concepts, properties, and relationships in problem-solving situations and communicate the reasoning used in solving these problems.

- Identify, classify, describe, and compare models of the two- and three-dimensional geometric figures previously identified.
- Use a construction tool to construct parallel line segments and parallelograms.
- Demonstrate how a change in shape affects area and/or perimeter.
- Use a grid to recreate two-dimensional figures of a given shape, area, and perimeter (circle, triangle, square, or rectangle) and determine its area and perimeter.

Standard 5 – Measurement

Students use a variety of tools and techniques to measure, apply the results in problem-solving situations, and communicate the reasoning used in solving these problems.

- Estimate and measure length (yards and meters), area, capacity (milliliters and liters), weight (gram and kilogram), time (minute intervals), and temperature (Fahrenheit) using standard units of measurement with an understanding of the results.
- Demonstrate the process of measuring length, time, temperature, and money, and explain the concepts related to the units of measurement.
- Without using measuring tools, know the approximate measures of familiar objects in U.S. and metric units and be able to use that information in a given situation (for example: the width of a finger, the temperature of a room, the weight of a hammer).

FOURTH GRADE

Standard 6 – Computation

Students link concepts and procedures as they develop and use computational techniques, including estimation, mental arithmetic, paper and pencil, calculators, and computers in problem-solving situations and communicate the reasoning used in solving these problems.

- ❏ Demonstrate conceptual meanings for addition, subtraction, multiplication, and division operations using whole numbers.

- ❏ Demonstrate the conceptual meaning for order and equivalency of fractions and decimals using physical models (including but not limited to money, unifix cubes, and other manipulative counters).

- ❏ Develop procedures for computing and estimating with whole numbers using the four basic arithmetic operations.

- ❏ Select and use appropriate methods for computing with whole numbers in problem-solving situations from among mental arithmetic, estimations, pencil-and-paper algorithms, and calculator or other mechanical methods in the four basic arithmetic operations.

 # SCIENCE

Standard 1 – Scientific Investigation

Students understand the processes of scientific investigation and design as well as conduct, communicate about, and evaluate such investigations.

- ❏ Individually, ask questions and state predictions (hypotheses) that can be addressed through scientific investigation.

- ❏ Individually, select and use simple devices to gather data related to an investigation.

- ❏ Access information using a variety of printed texts and electronic media.

- ❏ Organize observations through writing, drawing, graphing, oral presentations, and charts.

4 Fourth Grade

Standard 2 – Physical Science
Students understand common properties, forms, and changes in matter and energy (with a focus on physics and chemistry).

- Examine, describe, classify, and compare tangible objects in terms of common physical properties (for example: state of matter, size, shape, texture, flexibility, color).

- Make observations and gather data on quantities associated with energy, movement, and change (for example: distances for a bean-launcher, time for melting ice cube).

- Compare quantities associated with energy movement and change by constructing simple diagrams or charts (for example: graph of launch distances, chart of melting time).

- Describe an observed change (for example: a melting ice cube, crystal growth, burning candle, physical breakage) in terms of starting conditions, type of change, and ending conditions, using words, diagrams, or graphs.

Standard 3 – Life Science
Students understand the characteristics and structure of living things, the processes of life, and how living things interact with each other and their environment (with a focus on biology, anatomy, physiology, botany, zoology, ecology).

- Identify digestive, respiratory, and circulatory systems of the human body.

- Describe the basic food requirements for humans as summarized in the nutrition pyramid.

- Describe life cycles of selected organisms (for example: frog, chicken, butterfly, radish, bean plant).

- Observe and investigate human skeletal and muscle systems.

FOURTH GRADE

Standard 4 – Earth and Space Science
Students understand the processes and interactions of Earth's systems and the structure and dynamics of Earth and other objects in space (with a focus on geology, meteorology, astronomy, oceanography).

- ❑ Describe different types and uses of Earth materials (rocks, soil, minerals).
- ❑ Recognize that fossils are evidence of past life.
- ❑ Identify major features of Earth's surface (mountains, rivers, plains, hills, oceans, plateaus).
- ❑ Describe natural processes that change Earth's surface (weathering, erosion, mountain building, volcanic activity).

Standard 5 – Science, Technology, and Human Activity
Students understand interrelationships among science, technology, and human activity and how they can affect the world.

- ❑ Recognize the diversity of resources provided by Earth and the sun (soil, fuels, minerals, medicines, food).
- ❑ Identify careers that use science and technology.
- ❑ Describe and define the invention process (brainstorm, analyze, combine, and create).
- ❑ Describe the effects of pollution on the environment and suggest activities designed to conserve natural resources.

Standard 6 – Scientific Concepts
Students understand that science involves a particular way of knowing and understanding common connections among scientific disciplines.

- ❑ Recognize that when a science experiment is repeated with the same conditions, the experiment generally works the same way.
- ❑ Identify observable patterns and changes in their lives and predict future events based on those patterns.
- ❑ Describe and compare the components and interrelationships of a simple system.
- ❑ Compare knowledge gained from direct and indirect experience.

FOURTH GRADE

GEOGRAPHY

Standard 1 – People, Places, and Environments
Students know how to use and construct maps, globes, and other geographic tools to locate and derive information about people, places, and environments.

- Use graph coordinates to locate local cities and sites.
- Interpret map information using legend, scale, index.
- Graph counties and commodities of their state.
- Identify mountains, rivers, plains, plateaus, valleys, and the Continental Divide.
- Identify examples of the movement of goods, services, and ideas of people in relation to place.
- Explain why forts are beside rivers, farms are beside water supplies, ranches are where grazing is available, supply towns are at the base of mountains, mining towns are in mountains, etc.

Standard 2 – Regional Characteristics
Students know the physical and human characteristics of places, and use this knowledge to define and study regions and their patterns of change.

- Identify impact by people on changes in a local region.
- Identify regions: mountains, plains, plateaus, life zones (plains, foothills, montane, subalpine, alpine) and how these regions were affected by overgrazing, farming, mining, deforestation, and urbanization.

Standard 3 – Earth
Students understand how physical processes shape Earth's surface patterns and systems.

- Examine life zones in their state, differentiating between plants and animals in each zone.
- Compare and contrast life zones, giving examples of plants and animals in each zone.

Fourth Grade

Standard 4 – Economic, Political, Cultural, and Social Processes

Students understand how economic, political, cultural, and social processes interact to shape patterns of human populations, interdependence, cooperation, and conflict.

- ❑ Examine the cause of human migration.
- ❑ Compare and contrast Native American cultures.
- ❑ Examine Spanish American culture.
- ❑ Describe conflicts over land use in American history.

Standard 5 – Human Interactions

Students understand the effects of interactions between human and physical systems and the changes in meaning, use, distribution, and importance of resources.

- ❑ Discuss farming, mining, recreation, reservoirs, and other types of land use.
- ❑ Discuss how natural resources positively or negatively affect people.
- ❑ Discuss the use of land for state and national parks.
- ❑ Identify the distribution of resources.

Standard 6 – Past, Present, and Future

Students apply knowledge of people, places, and environments to understand the past and present and to plan for the future.

- ❑ Describe how mining or farming areas have changed over time.
- ❑ Compare and contrast early residents in relation to geographical location.

Fourth Grade

HISTORY

Standard 1 – Chronological Organization
Students understand the chronological organization of history and know how to organize events and people into major eras to identify and explain historical relationships.

- Prepare a time line accurately depicting significant people and events in their state history, using correct sequence.
- Select two groups from their state history who had a conflict with each other, and describe the cause and effect of the conflict.

Standard 2 – Historical Inquiry
Students know how to use the processes and resources of historical inquiry.

- Compile information into a research report (either written or oral).
- Describe the oral tradition of sharing culture from generation to generation.

Standard 3 – Diverse Societies
Students understand that societies are diverse and have changed over time.

- Recognize significant contributions of various groups of people who settled in their state.

Standard 4 – Science, Technology, and Economic Activity
Students understand how science, technology, and economic activity have developed, changed, and affected societies throughout history.

- Compare the lives of hunters and gatherers to the lives of people who cultivated plants and raised domesticated animals for food.
- Describe the impact of various technological developments on the local community and the state (for example: irrigation, transportation, communication).
- Describe the economic reasons why people move to or from a location.
- Discuss the development of towns.
- Describe different systems of exchange that can be used.

FOURTH GRADE

Standard 5 – Political Institutions and Theories

Students understand political institutions and theories that have developed and changed over time.

- ❑ Describe their state as a political unit.
- ❑ Discuss the role of government leaders (for example: governor, mayor, state representatives, state senators, U.S. representatives, and U.S. senators).
- ❑ Give examples of how individuals and/or various groups have gained, lost, or maintained political rights, freedoms, power, or cultural identity in the history of the community, region, or state.
- ❑ Describe contributions of family members in local history.

Standard 6 – Religion and Philosophy

Students know that religious and philosophical ideas have been powerful forces throughout history.

- ❑ Describe traditions based on cultural beliefs and ideas.
- ❑ Give examples of how beliefs of the people are reflected in the celebrations and practices of their community.
- ❑ Give examples of forms of expression that depict the history, daily life, and beliefs of various peoples (for example: folk tales, ballads, dance, and architecture).

FIFTH GRADE

Language Arts
Math
Science
Geography
History

PARENTS' GUIDE TO STANDARDS

5 FIFTH GRADE

 LANGUAGE ARTS

Standard 1 – Reading
Students read and understand a variety of materials.

- Use comprehension strategies: preview, predict and confirm, compare and contrast.
- Connect reading with personal experience and background knowledge.
- Use information from reading to increase vocabulary.

Standard 2 – Writing and Speaking
Students write and speak for a variety of purposes and audiences.

- Organize ideas into draft form.
- Communicate effectively through oral presentation to an audience.
- Provide basic supporting information.
- Do guided pre-writing (for example: brainstorming, webbing, etc.)
- Demonstrate basic understanding of the following organizational strategies: lists, webs, story maps, brainstorming.
- Vary word choices by using devices such as synonyms and antonyms, descriptive language, figures of speech (for example: simile and metaphor).
- Produce oral presentations demonstrating effective use of notes, adequate voice volume and enunciation, and eye contact with audience.

Standard 3 – Language Structure
Students write and speak using conventional grammar, usage, sentence structure, punctuation, capitalization, and spelling.

- Use appropriate end punctuation in sentences.
- Correctly use common regular and irregular verb forms in context.
- Correctly punctuate singular possessives.

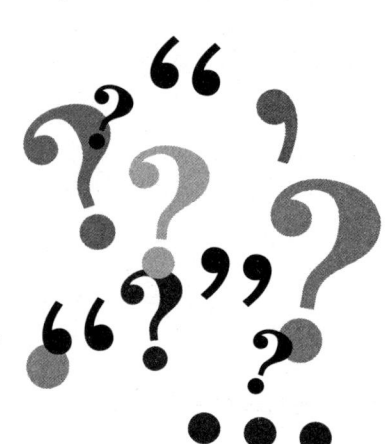

FIFTH GRADE

Standard 4 – Thinking and Viewing

Students apply thinking skills to their reading, writing, speaking, listening, and viewing.

- ❑ Make predictions.
- ❑ Draw conclusions.
- ❑ Identify the problem in a given work.
- ❑ Develop possible solutions to a problem.
- ❑ Develop reasons to support a personal point of view.
- ❑ Begin to identify the historical and cultural influences in a work.

Standard 5 – Research

Students read to locate, select, and make use of relevant information from a variety of media, reference, and technological sources.

- ❑ Focus on appropriate questions and identify likely resources.
- ❑ Locate specific information using computer card catalog, table of contents in a book, and index in a book.
- ❑ State information from a resource in their own words.
- ❑ Give credit for borrowed information in a simplified bibliography format, with teacher assistance.

Standard 6 – Literature and Culture

Students read and recognize literature as a record and expression of cultural heritage.

- ❑ Identify setting, plot, and main character in a story.
- ❑ Differentiate between fiction and nonfiction.
- ❑ Read, respond to, and discuss a variety of literature as it connects to personal experience and cultural background.
- ❑ Read, respond to, and discuss historical fiction reflecting United States history.

Fifth Grade

 **Math**

Standard 1 – Number Sense
Students develop number sense, use numbers and number relationships in problem-solving situations, and communicate the reasoning used in solving these problems.

- ❏ Locate and order decimals and common fractions on the number line.
- ❏ Read, write, order, and compare integers, rational numbers, and simple irrational numbers.
- ❏ Find multiples and least common multiples.
- ❏ Identify the relationships among the concepts of fractions, decimal numbers, and division.

Standard 2 – Patterns and Algebra
Students use algebraic methods to explore, model, and describe patterns and functions involving numbers, shapes, data, and graphs in problem-solving situations and communicate the reasoning used in solving these problems.

- ❏ Recognize and extend simple geometric patterns with tiles.
- ❏ Model integers with manipulatives.
- ❏ Recognize the change that occurs with division (for example: decrease in divisor results in an increase in quotient).
- ❏ Recognize linear relationships (for example: if one candy bar costs $.50, then two candy bars cost $1.00).

Standard 3 – Statistics and Probability
Students use data collection and analysis, statistics, and probability in problem-solving situations and communicate the reasoning used in solving these problems.

- ❏ Read, interpret, and construct line and bar graphs using the concept of varied scale and axis.
- ❏ Conduct and interpret surveys.
- ❏ Make predictions and compare results using experimental probability of one variable.
- ❏ Draw simple tree diagrams to determine possible outcomes of combinations of two or more variables.

Standard 4 – Geometry

Students use geometric concepts, properties, and relationships in problem-solving situations and communicate the reasoning used in solving these problems.

- ❑ Know properties and vocabulary of quadrilaterals, squares, rectangles, parallelograms, circles, and triangles.

- ❑ Construct two-dimensional models of squares, rectangles, triangles, and circles using a variety of methods and tools.

- ❑ Demonstrate concept of perimeter and area of two-dimensional figures.

Standard 5 – Measurement

Students use a variety of tools and techniques to measure, apply the results in problem-solving situations, and communicate the reasoning used in solving these problems.

- ❑ Estimate and measure the perimeter and area of squares, rectangles, and triangles.

- ❑ Identify the standard of measurement of unit capacity, weight, and mass, using both U.S. and metric measurements (no conversions).

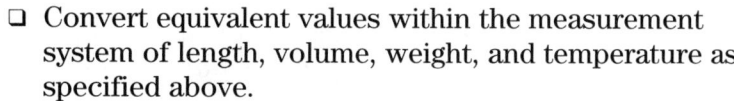

- ❑ Estimate and use tools to measure within the measurement systems of length (m, dm, cm, mm, yards, feet, inches, and ½ inch), volume (liters, ml, cups, pints, quarts, and gallons), weight (grams, kg, and pounds) and temperature (Fahrenheit and Celsius).

- ❑ Convert equivalent values within the measurement system of length, volume, weight, and temperature as specified above.

- ❑ Use area and perimeter formulas to calculate the area and perimeters of squares and rectangles.

FIFTH GRADE

Standard 6 – Computation

Students link concepts and procedures as they develop and use computational techniques, including estimation, mental arithmetic, paper and pencil, calculators, and computers, in problem-solving situations and communicate the reasoning used in solving these problems.

- ❑ Use the estimation techniques of rounding, truncating, and educated guessing based on prior information.

- ❑ Demonstrate proficiency in multi-digit addition and subtraction with regrouping; multi-digit multiplication (four digits by two digits), and division (two digit by one digit with remainder).

- ❑ Select and use appropriate methods for computing with whole numbers and commonly used fractions, decimals, and percents in problem-solving situations from among mental arithmetic, estimations, pencil-and-paper algorithms, and calculator or other mechanical methods in the four basic arithmetic operations.

- ❑ Calculate least common multiples, greatest common factors, and equivalent fractions for very simple fractions (denominators of 2, 3, 4).

- ❑ Explain ratio and proportion from a physical model.

SCIENCE

Standard 1 – Scientific Investigation

Students understand the processes of scientific investigation and design as well as conduct, communicate about, and evaluate such investigations.

- ❑ Organize and analyze data from experiments and investigations, and relate laboratory studies to natural systems.

- ❑ Set up experiments to study cause-and-effect relationships.

- ❑ Compare outcomes of experiments.

- ❑ Communicate work in various ways: written reports, oral presentations, graphs, charts, spreadsheets, art work.

Standard 2 – Physical Science

Students understand common properties, forms, and changes in matter and energy (with a focus on physics and chemistry).

- ❏ Predict outcomes by changing variables.
- ❏ Design and conduct experiments using simple machines (for example: pendulums, catapults, pulleys, levers).
- ❏ Measure force, distance, and work involved using levers and pulleys.
- ❏ Identify and classify factors causing change within a system.

Standard 3 – Life Science

Students understand the characteristics and structure of living things, the processes of life, and how living things interact with each other and their environment (with a focus on biology, anatomy, physiology, botany, zoology, ecology).

- ❏ Based on attributes, place living organisms into groups based on similarities.
- ❏ Identify living and nonliving components of an ecosystem when given an example of one.
- ❏ Identify the characteristics of healthy, functioning ecosystems.
- ❏ Explain the interaction and interdependence of nonliving and living components within ecosystems.

Standard 4 – Earth and Space Science

Students understand the processes and interactions of Earth's systems and the structure and dynamics of Earth and other objects in space (with a focus on geology, meteorology, astronomy, oceanography).

- ❏ Explain the H_2O cycle and identify sources of fresh and salt H_2O.
- ❏ Describe differences in salt and fresh water (salinity).
- ❏ Explore uses of water in production of energy.

Fifth Grade

Standard 5 – Science, Technology, and Human Activity

Students understand interrelationships among science, technology, and human activity and how they can affect the world.

- ❑ Identify renewable and nonrenewable resources.
- ❑ Categorize the types of science and technology used in various careers.
- ❑ Recognize that technologies consume and generate energy.
- ❑ Know that designing a solution to a simple problem may have constraints, such as cost, materials, time, space, and safety.

Standard 6 – Scientific Concepts

Students understand that science involves a particular way of knowing and understand common connections among scientific disciplines.

- ❑ Give examples of how scientific knowledge changes as new knowledge is acquired.
- ❑ Explain why the same experiment must have comparable results when repeated.
- ❑ Identify variables related to change.
- ❑ Know that women and men of all ages, backgrounds, and groups participate in the various areas of science and technology, as they have for many centuries.

FIFTH GRADE 5

GEOGRAPHY

Standard 1 – People, Places, and Environments
Students know how to use and construct maps, globes, and other geographic tools to locate and derive information about people, places, and environments.

- ❑ Use contour and aerial photography maps.
- ❑ Use the atlas as a tool to understand products, maps, and commodities map of U.S.
- ❑ Construct maps for different periods in U.S. history.
- ❑ Identify and locate physical and human features in the United States as they relate to each unit.

Standard 2 – Regional Characteristics
Students know the physical and human characteristics of places, and use this knowledge to define and study regions and their patterns of change.

- ❑ Describe the characteristics of places that occur naturally or are made by people in the major study units.
- ❑ Identify the distinguishing characteristics of the major regions in the Colonial Period (New England, Middle, and Southern colonies).
- ❑ Examine the industrialization of the Northeast with water power, technological changes, and lack of fertile soil.
- ❑ Analyze the events of North vs. South vs. West during the expansion of the nation.

- ❑ Explain how culture and technology affect the way people perceive places and regions.
- ❑ Explain how places and regions serve as cultural symbols.

Fifth Grade

Standard 3 – Earth
Students understand how physical processes shape Earth's surface patterns and systems.

- Examine landforms, deltas, flood plains, and canyons.
- Examine the effects of mountains on the westward movement of settlers crossing the great American desert to get to Oregon.

Standard 4 – Economic, Political, Cultural, and Social Processes
Students understand how economic, political, cultural, and social processes interact to shape patterns of human populations, interdependence, cooperation, and conflict.

- Understand reasons why settlement stopped at the Appalachian Mountains.
- Note differences between New England, Middle, and Southern colonies.
- Examine how the colonies traded raw materials for manufactured goods from England.
- Understand the importance of river highways, ocean travel, canals, and railroads in moving goods.
- Understand how canals and railroads influenced the importance of certain cities.
- Examine the pattern of settlements following rivers.
- Examine the cooperation and conflict among people on wagon trains during the westward movement period.

Standard 5 – Human Interactions
Students understand the effects of interactions between human and physical systems and the changes in meaning, use, distribution, and importance of resources.

- Explain the role of steamships, canals, and railroads in the development of towns and industries.
- Describe how the cotton gin led to huge plantations.
- Describe how natural events affect human activities.
- Understand the importance of water on the Oregon Trail.
- Understand the Native American view of land ownership vs. the European view of land ownership.

Standard 6 – Past, Present, and Future

Students apply knowledge of people, places, and environments to understand the past and present and to plan for the future.

❑ Analyze how the Oregon Territory affected the westward movement.

HISTORY

Standard 1 – Chronological Organization

Students understand the chronological organization of history and know how to organize events and people into major eras to identify and explain historical relationships.

❑ Put in chronological order important people and events in major study units.

❑ Understand the influence that England, France, Spain, and their colonies had on U.S. history.

❑ Read primary, secondary, and historical fiction sources and write a response that includes a sequence of the events.

❑ Examine the ways that people made a living and identify those ways in each major study unit.

Standard 2 – Historical Inquiry

Students know how to use the processes and resources of historical inquiry.

❑ Read primary and secondary sources and formulate questions.

❑ Determine if the information gathered is sufficient to answer historical questions.

❑ Find information revealed through artifacts; read to find additional details and discuss.

❑ Examine the relationship between current events and important history themes.

Fifth Grade

Standard 3 – Diverse Societies

Students understand that societies are diverse and have changed over time.

- Identify the common traits and characteristics that unite the United States as a nation and a society.
- Explain why people and cultures have come to live in the Americas.
- Identify and give examples of the basic elements of cultural and social organization in the major study units.
- Describe how social roles, traditions, and the characteristics of social organization have both changed and endured in the United States throughout its history.

Standard 4 – Science, Technology, and Economic Activity

Students understand how science, technology, and economic activity have developed, changed, and affected societies throughout history.

- Explain the significance of scientific development during each major study unit.
- Examine how changes in transportation affected the settlement of the U.S. (for example: steamboats, roads, and canals).
- Examine how inventions affected people's lives.
- Explain how mineral resources and water played a major role in the settlement of the West.
- Explain how the triangle trade affected slavery.
- Describe historical events and the role of individuals in the economic development.

Standard 5 – Political Institutions and Theories

Students understand political institutions and theories that have developed and changed over time.

- ❏ Learn the principles of self government, representative government, and individual rights.
- ❏ Learn the basic ideas set forth in the Declaration of Independence, Constitution, and Bill of Rights.
- ❏ Describe how political rights have been affected by, but not limited to, gender, race, national origin, and religion.
- ❏ Describe how the use of military power influenced the political history of the U.S. (for example: Revolutionary War, Civil War, and war with the Native Americans).

Standard 6 – Religion and Philosophy

Students know that religious and philosophical ideas have been powerful forces throughout history.

- ❏ Identify the religious differences between the Southern, Middle, and New England colonies.
- ❏ Understand that the freedom of religion principle in the U.S. allowed many religions to flourish.
- ❏ Give and describe examples of individuals who, throughout history, acted from their religious or philosophical beliefs.
- ❏ Examine art forms of various ethnic groups in the U.S.
- ❏ Understand how literature reflects American traditions.
- ❏ Discuss the significance of various U. S. structures (for example: Capitol, Statue of Liberty, Lincoln Memorial).

Sixth Grade

Language Arts
Math
Science
Geography
History

Parents' Guide to Standards

SIXTH GRADE

LANGUAGE ARTS

Standard 1 – Reading
Students read and understand a variety of materials.

- Use comprehension strategies such as re-read, summarize, determine main idea, and apply knowledge of similes and other figures of speech.
- Use word-recognition strategies such as word order clues (transition words) and dictionary skills.
- Use word parts (roots, prefixes, suffixes) to increase vocabulary.
- Use information from their reading to increase vocabulary.

Standard 2 – Writing and Speaking
Students write and speak for a variety of purposes and audiences.

- Write to explain, inform, entertain, or express.
- Select topics reflecting established purpose.
- Edit and revise with guidance.
- Use organization tools in preparing oral presentations.

Standard 3 – Language Structure
Students write and speak using conventional grammar, usage, sentence structure, punctuation, capitalization, and spelling.

- Demonstrate guided and independent use of homonyms and homophones in writing and speaking.
- Correctly punctuate and capitalize story and book titles in their writing.
- Correctly spell commonly used words.

Standard 4 – Thinking and Viewing
Students apply thinking skills to their reading, writing, speaking, listening, and viewing.

- Practice identifying cause and effect.
- Identify likenesses and differences.
- Discuss solutions and consequences.
- Begin to identify the historical and cultural influences in a work.

Sixth Grade

Standard 5 – Research

Students read to locate, select, and make use of relevant information from a variety of media, reference, and technological sources.

- Locate specific information using glossaries, alphabetical or numerical arrangement of topics, keyword search, and electronic media.
- State information from a resource in their own words.
- Give credit for borrowed information in a simplified bibliography format, with teacher assistance.
- Use information from research in an end product (written, oral, visual, or multimedia).

Standard 6 – Literature and Culture

Students read and recognize literature as a record and expression of cultural heritage.

- Identify conflict and mood in a story.
- Recognize autobiography, biography, and poetry.
- Read, respond to, and discuss a variety of literature as it connects to personal experience and cultural background.
- Read, respond to, and discuss literature as a way to explore similarities and differences among cultures.

SIXTH GRADE

 MATH

Standard 1 – Number Sense
Students develop number sense, use numbers and number relationships in problem-solving situations, and communicate the reasoning used in solving these problems.

- Use physical materials and number lines to demonstrate integers, rational numbers, and percents.
- Identify other base systems.
- Identify pi (π) and exponents, specifically squares.
- Read, write, compare, and order integers and positive rational numbers.
- Find least common multiple and greatest common factor.
- Make factor trees.
- Use Venn diagrams to demonstrate groupings.
- Identify the relationships among the concepts of fractions, decimal numbers, and division.

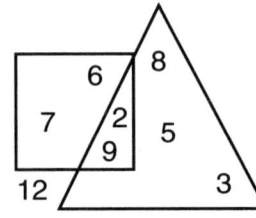

Standard 2 – Patterns and Algebra
Students use algebraic methods to explore, model, and describe patterns and functions involving numbers, shapes, data, and graphs in problem-solving situations and communicate the reasoning used in solving these problems.

- Recognize more complex models of geometric patterns.
- Recognize how scale affects interpretation of a graph.
- Verbalize a rule from a modeled pattern.
- Demonstrate one- and two-step equations with physical models (for example: a balance scale).
- Recognize that a variable can represent an unknown in an equation, and apply in simple problem-solving situation.
- Use variables in formulas to solve a problem.
- Predict and state the differences in the changes that occur in linear and nonlinear relationships (example: $y = x$, $y = x^2$).

Sixth Grade

Standard 3 – Statistics and Probability

Students use data collection and analysis, statistics, and probability in problem-solving situations and communicate the reasoning used in solving these problems.

- ❏ Define and use the terms *mean*, *median*, and *mode*.
- ❏ Calculate averages using whole numbers and decimals.
- ❏ Make predictions and compare results using experimental probability with two variables.
- ❏ Use simple grids and tree diagrams to find all possible outcomes.

Standard 4 – Geometry

Students use geometric concepts, properties, and relationships in problem-solving situations and communicate the reasoning used in solving these problems.

- ❏ Know and be able to describe the properties and vocabulary of plane geometry (including lines, line segments, rays, angles, polygons, circles, parallelism, perpendicularity, congruence, and similarity).
- ❏ Construct physical models of prisms, pyramids, cones, cylinders, and spheres.
- ❏ Take apart a three-dimensional model and return it to a two-dimensional figure that shows all the faces of the original three-dimensional model.
- ❏ Draw a Cartesian coordinate grid and label the axes, origin, and quadrants.
- ❏ Plot ordered pairs on a coordinate grid that includes positive and negative values on both axes.
- ❏ Calculate the surface area and volume of a cube from a physical model.

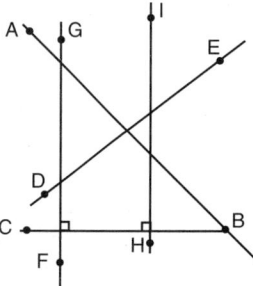

SIXTH GRADE

Standard 5 – Measurement

Students use a variety of tools and techniques to measure, apply the results in problem-solving situations, and communicate the reasoning used in solving these problems.

- ❏ Estimate and measure length using m, cm, mm, yd, ft, in, ½ in, and ¼ in.
- ❏ Estimate and measure the perimeter and area of squares, rectangles, triangles, and circles.
- ❏ Use formulas to calculate the perimeter and area of squares, rectangles, triangles, and circles.
- ❏ Illustrate and model with manipulatives how the change of linear dimension affects perimeter, area, and volume.

Standard 6 – Computation

Students link concepts and procedures as they develop and use computational techniques, including estimation, mental arithmetic, paper and pencil, calculators, and computers, in problem-solving situations and communicate the reasoning used in solving these problems.

- ❏ Estimate operations from whole number, decimal, fraction, mixed number, and integer computations in problem-solving situations.
- ❏ Demonstrate proficiency with paper-and-pencil computations, estimation, and mental arithmetic over the set of rational numbers.
- ❏ Demonstrate proficiency of converting mixed numbers and improper fractions using models and paper-and-pencil calculations.
- ❏ Demonstrate proficiency of converting fractions to decimals and percents.

SIXTH GRADE

SCIENCE

Standard 1 – Scientific Investigation
Students understand the processes of scientific investigation and design as well as conduct, communicate about, and evaluate such investigations.

- ❏ Use appropriate tools to measure (for example: balances and weights, meter sticks, graduated cylinders, beakers, thermometers).

- ❏ Follow a plan to conduct a scientific investigation that involves questions, hypothesis, controlling variables, collecting data, drawing conclusions, and making predictions.

- ❏ Communicate with oral or written reports, graphs, charts, spreadsheets, and art.

- ❏ Establish relationships based on evidence and logical argument (provides causes for effects).

Standard 2 – Physical Science
Students understand common properties, forms, and changes in matter and energy (with a focus on physics and chemistry).

- ❏ Observe solar energy transfer.

- ❏ Design simple models that demonstrate temperature transformation (for example: solar water heaters, solar space heaters).

- ❏ Measure quantities associated with energy forms (for example: mass, temperature).

- ❏ Understand that energy moves in predictable ways, flowing from warmer objects to cooler ones until both objects are at the same temperature.

Sixth Grade

Standard 3 – Life Science

Students understand the characteristics and structure of living things, the processes of life, and how living things interact with each other and their environment (with a focus on biology, anatomy, physiology, botany, zoology, ecology).

- ❑ Identify the components, relationships, and processes necessary to maintain an ecosystem.

- ❑ Categorize organisms according to their roles in food chains and webs.

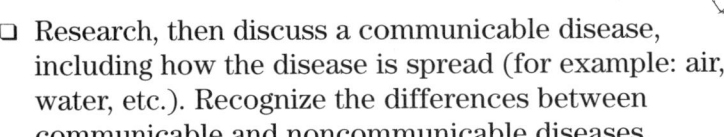

- ❑ Explain the interdependence of body systems to the survival of the organism.

- ❑ Research, then discuss a communicable disease, including how the disease is spread (for example: air, water, etc.). Recognize the differences between communicable and noncommunicable diseases.

Standard 4 – Earth and Space Science

Students understand the processes and interactions of Earth's systems and the structure and dynamics of Earth and other objects in space (with a focus on geology, meteorology, astronomy, oceanography).

Not addressed at this level.

Standard 5 – Science, Technology, and Human Activity

Students understand interrelationships among science, technology, and human activity and how they can affect the world.

- ❑ Investigate current trends in the consumption of renewable and nonrenewable resources worldwide.

- ❑ Identify and explore a technological industry's use of science and technology in that field.

- ❑ Identify and explore new technologies and how these new technologies affect the environment.

- ❑ Know that a technological design should meet criteria established in the original purpose.

Sixth Grade

Standard 6 – Scientific Concepts

Students understand that science involves a particular way of knowing and understanding common connections among scientific disciplines.

- ❏ Identify variables and conditions related to change.
- ❏ Use a model to describe an event.
- ❏ Identify and compare today's technologies with those of their parents and grandparents.
- ❏ Know that women and men of diverse interests, talents, qualities, and motivations, and of various social and ethnic backgrounds, engage in the activities of science, engineering, and related fields; some scientists work in teams, some work alone, but all communicate with others.

GEOGRAPHY

Standard 1 – People, Places, and Environments

Students know how to use and construct maps, globes, and other geographic tools to locate and derive information about people, places, and environments.

- ❏ Understand map keys showing elevation, population, economics, and population density.
- ❏ Use atlas, text, and technology to understand and compare various maps.
- ❏ Use maps to identify physical and human features of North America in terms of location, distance between locations, size, and population density.
- ❏ Describe the patterns and processes of migration and the spread of ideas, people, technology, and products among places.
- ❏ Discuss interaction between bordering countries.

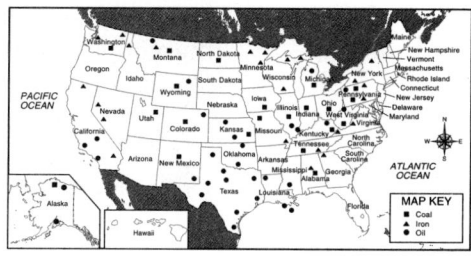

Sixth Grade

Standard 2 – Regional Characteristics

Students know the physical and human characteristics of places, and use this knowledge to define and study regions and their patterns of change.

- Identify and compare physical and human characteristics of North America (for example: largest cities, historic sites, landforms, rivers).
- Recognize perceptions people have of an area based on its physical characteristics and cultural history.
- Determine how ancient cultures and religions affect present-day people.

Standard 3 – Earth

Students understand how physical processes shape Earth's surface patterns and systems.

- Explain how physical processes, such as water and ice or volcanoes and earthquakes, produce distinctive landforms.
- Examine the processes that produce renewable and nonrenewable resources and their economic potential.
- Compare and contrast local ecosystem patterns with those in various locations of North America.
- Examine and be able to compare and contrast the ecosystems of North America as they affect and pertain to areas of study.

Standard 4 – Economic, Political, Cultural, and Social Processes

Students understand how economic, political, cultural, and social processes interact to shape patterns of human populations, interdependence, cooperation, and conflict.

- Determine the various ethnic groups that make up the population of North America and use a variety of visual materials, data sources, and narratives to describe the human characteristics of a region and compare them to characteristics of surrounding regions.
- Explain why and how countries trade goods and services.
- Understand land use possibilities that determine the economic value of a region.

- Use graphs, charts, and data-retrieval sources to show that job opportunities lead to migration of people from one area to another.
- Understand the reasons for conflict and cooperation among people as they set about inhabiting a particular region.

Standard 5 – Human Interactions

Students understand the effects of interactions between human and physical systems and the changes in meaning, use, distribution, and importance of resources.

- Describe the influence of transportation systems on the development of North America.
- Describe how earthquakes and floods affect human activities.
- Understand the reasons for and economic impact of import and export to and from a particular region.
- Identify how technology affects the definition of, access to, and use of resources.

Standard 6 – Past, Present, and Future

Students apply knowledge of people, places, and environments to understand the past and present and to plan for the future.

- Understand how a group of people adapted to climate, landforms, etc.
- Understand how geographic features affect interactions between the peoples of North America.

SIXTH GRADE

HISTORY

Standard 1 – Chronological Organization
Students understand the chronological organization of history and know how to organize events and people into major eras to identify and explain historical relationships.

- ❏ Organize major historical events of Canada and Mexico.

- ❏ Read primary and secondary historical fiction sources and write a response that includes a sequence of the events about Canada and/or Mexico.

- ❏ Examine the role of economics and technology in the domination of Europeans in North America, specifically Canada and Mexico, in the 17th and 18th centuries.

Standard 2 – Historical Inquiry
Students know how to use the processes and resources of historical inquiry.

- ❏ Read primary and secondary sources on Canada and Mexico and look at the issues of cause and effect.

- ❏ Identify which sources are primary and secondary when reading about researching Canada and Mexico.

- ❏ Examine historical events in Canada and Mexico and relate them to the present.

Standard 3 – Diverse Societies
Students understand that societies are diverse and have changed over time.

- ❏ Identify the contributions of the early cultures in Canada and Mexico.

- ❏ Examine the Aztecs and Mayans and their interaction with the Spanish.

Standard 4 – Science, Technology, and Economic Activity

Students understand how science, technology, and economic activity have developed, changed, and affected societies throughout history.

- ❏ Describe the roles of mercantilism and transportation as they relate to European influence in Canada and Mexico.

- ❏ Examine the trade relationships between Canada, the United States, and Mexico.

Standard 5 – Political Institutions and Theories

Students understand political institutions and theories that have developed and changed over time.

- ❏ Describe the basic type of government in both Canada and Mexico.

- ❏ Describe how the use of military power has influenced the political history of Canada and Mexico.

- ❏ Identify the key political alliances in the Americas (for example: NAFTA, OAS).

Standard 6 – Religion and Philosophy

Students know that religious and philosophical ideas have been powerful forces throughout history.

- ❏ Examine the role of philosophical and religious leaders in the fight for independence in Mexico and Canada (for example: Father Hidalgo, Morelos, Zapata, Nellie McClung, William Lyon Mackenzie).

- ❏ Examine the art and music of Canada and Mexico.

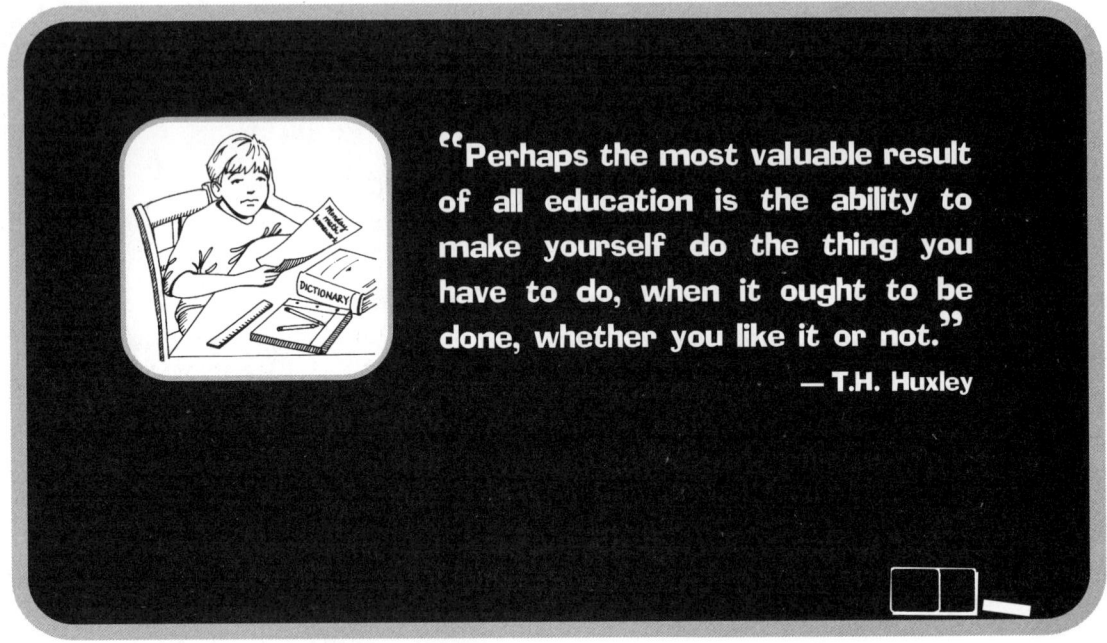